THEY WILL NEVER
BE FORGOTTEN

SANDRA LEAH

WESTBOW
PRESS®
A DIVISION OF THOMAS NELSON
& ZONDERVAN

WestBow Press books may be ordered through booksellers or by contacting:

WestBow Press
A Division of Thomas Nelson & Zondervan
1663 Liberty Drive
Bloomington, IN 47403
www.westbowpress.com
844-714-3454

Because of the dynamic nature of the Internet, any web addresses or links contained in this book may have changed since publication and may no longer be valid. The views expressed in this work are solely those of the author and do not necessarily reflect the views of the publisher, and the publisher hereby disclaims any responsibility for them.

Scripture taken from the Holy Bible, NEW INTERNATIONAL VERSION®. Copyright © 1973, 1978, 1984 by Biblica, Inc. All rights reserved worldwide. Used by permission. NEW INTERNATIONAL VERSION® and NIV® are registered trademarks of Biblica, Inc. Use of either trademark for the offering of goods or services requires the prior written consent of Biblica US, Inc.

Any people depicted in stock imagery provided by Thinkstock are models, and such images are being used for illustrative purposes only. Certain stock imagery © Thinkstock.

ISBN: 978-1-4908-9956-5 (sc)
ISBN: 978-1-4908-9958-9 (hc)
ISBN: 978-1-4908-9957-2 (e)

Library of Congress Control Number: 2015918901

Print information available on the last page.

WestBow Press rev. date: 11/11/2015

CONTENTS

I dedicate this book to my daughter Lisa, who went on part of this journey with me, and in remembrance to my son Eric.

A special "thank you" to Michelle my assistant who accepted the challenge of translating my handwriting and helping organize this book. Also, my granddaughter Christina who at age 14 provided all the angel artwork and scanned the pictures.

PREFACE

This book is written in memory of my son, who taught me that with love, and a great deal of faith, we can move on in life after the loss of a loved one. He taught me to be strong and never give up. Because of his great courage and strength during his fight with cancer, his sister Lisa and I were able to go on with our lives. God also played a great role. It is because of Eric and God that I know this story has to be written.

Over the two and a half years of knowing I would lose my son, my thoughts were also led to Mother Mary. She too lost her son. She must have felt as I did, why my son? This book is a look at my life and a close look at Mother Mary's life. It is with God's help and my son's memory that I share with you my story and what I feel Mary's life would have been like.

This book is written to give strength and courage to people who have lost a loved one, who will lose a loved one, and to anyone who needs strength to carry on during a difficult time. Eric and God helped me, and I hope this book will also give strength to anyone reading it.

As I tell this story, I want to pay tribute to all the people that helped me during this time. I want you to open your mind and imagine, what I feel Mary's life was like. Her story is as I pictured it in my mind.

"Open up your heart, and he will be with you in your time of trouble." I learned from my son that our life has a reason and that death, with its sting, is a part of our life.

The following passages from the Bible, were given to me, as a gift from God. You will learn how this was given to me and how it helped with my healing.

But someone may ask, "How are the dead raised?" with what kind of body will they come? How foolish! What you sow does not come to life unless it dies. When you sow you do not plant the body that will be, but just a seed perhaps of wheat or of something else. But God gave it a body as he has determined, and to each kind of seed he gives its own body. All flesh is not the same. Men have one kind of flesh; animals have another, birds another, and fish another. There are also heavenly bodies and there are earthly bodies, but the splendor of the heavenly bodies is one kind and the splendor of the earthly bodies is another. The sun has one kind of splendor, the moon another and the stars another; and star differs from star in splendor.

So, will it be with the resurrection of the dead. The body that is sown is perishable. It is raised imperishable! It is sown in dishonor; it is raised in glory; it is sown in weakness. It is raised in power; it is sown a natural body, it is raised a spiritual body.

If there is a natural body, there is also a spiritual body. So, it is written: The first man Adam became a living being. The last Adam, a life giving spirit. The spiritual did not come first, but the natural and after that the spiritual. The first man of the dust of the earth, the second man from heaven. As was the earthly man. So, are those who are of the earth; and as is the man from heaven, so also are those who are of heaven. And just as we have been born in the likeness of the earthly man, so shall we bear the likeness of the man from heaven.

I declare to you brothers, that flesh and blood cannot inherit the kingdom of God, nor does the perishable inherit the imperishable. Listen, I tell you a mystery; we will not all sleep, but we will all be changed-in a flash, in the twinkle of an eye, at the last trumpet. For the trumpet will sound, the dead will be raised imperishable, and we will be changed. For the perishable must clothe itself with the imperishable and the mortal with immortality. When the perishable has been clothed with imperishable, and the mortal with immortality, then the saying that is written will come true;

"Death has been swallowed up in victory.
Where, Oh death is your victory?
Where, Oh death is your sting?
The sting of death is sin, and the power of sin is the law. But thanks be to God! He gives us the victory through our Lord Jesus Christ.

Therefore, my dear brothers, stand firm. Let nothing move you. Always give yourself fully to the work of the Lord, because you know that your labor in the Lord is not in vain.

(1 Corinthians 15: 35-58)

CHAPTER 1 A & B

"And God shall wipe away all tears from
their eyes and there shall be no more death
neither sorrow, nor crying, neither shall
there be any more pain for the former
things are passed away."

Revelations 21: 4

(June 29, 1995 – One year after Eric's passing)

As we drove down Mineral Point Road, I thought about the many times I had driven down this road. My daughter, Lisa, was driving and telling me about the many times she had gone to our destination. She told me I would be impressed with what I was about to see. As we made the turn and started down a one-way road, I looked around at all of the vases filled with flowers. The green grass reached out in all directions. Several large statues reached up to the blue sky. The peacefulness was all around us. As we made the last turn, I looked around for the tree that was the marker. Suddenly I saw the white flowers in the only vase in the green grassy area. The tree showed me his stone marker.

I could feel my insides building with a sudden pain and hurt. The crying I held back for a year could no longer be contained. I picked up the three wooden calla lilies that I had on my lap, and whispered to Lisa, "Please let me be alone with him." I walked toward the stone marker and I saw my son's name engraved.

Eric A. Haug 1969-1994

The marker had lilies, his favorite flowers, outlining it. The tears would not stop. I pushed some of the grass away and rearranged the white silk flowers in the vase. I picked up the three wooden calla lilies and added them to the others. One was from Lisa, one from his father, and one from his mother – me. I arranged them and then rearranged them; to make sure they were just perfect. When the Garden of Gethsemane was chosen, for the area where he would be laid to rest, I was at once reminded of Jesus and the time spent talking with his father, God in the same named garden.

I had waited the whole last year for this moment. I looked at the surroundings, the pine tree that would always tell me where he was laid to rest. The colored flowers surrounding in the other areas, the other gardens all had a statue in the center. The Garden of Gethsemane would also have a statue, in a few years. Eric was the first one to be laid to rest in this garden. His was the only marker, the only vase filled with flowers, in this quiet setting. I was sure that this would change in the future. I could hear a bird chirping in the background, a breeze danced through the tree above me, and peacefulness was everywhere. As I looked around, I could not stop crying. Something was bothering me. I came here to be with my son. However I felt this strange feeling within me. Then a great feeling grew up within my heart. Eric was not here!

I started speaking to him, "Eric, I waited so long to come and be with you, where are you?" Suddenly, a feeling of relief came over me. He was not here, all the time that had gone by, now only proved to me that he lived within me. In my memories, in the artwork he left behind, in the music he liked, and that I still listened to. In his voice I would always hear, but now no longer converse with his face that I would always remember.

All around me was beauty and calm and peacefulness in this Garden of Gethsemane, where he would always be laid to rest. My heart was now at peace. Eric's spirit would always be within me, never to be forgotten! Lisa walked up to me and I reached for her hand. We stood together for a few minutes in silence. We both were overwhelmed with sadness; we both missed him so much. As we turned to go my life flashed through my mind.

View of marker and he was the only one laid
to rest in the Garden of Gethsemane

(One year after the death of Jesus, possibly April 6, 33 A.D.)

Mary's sandals made a clicking noise, as she walked quickly down the cobblestone street. She had told John the Apostle to stay behind, as she came close to the tomb of Joseph of Arimathaea, where it is believed Jesus was entombed. The year had passed quickly and this was the day she had waited for. Many changes had happened in her life during the past year. In the Jewish religion, she was to go to the place of her son's tomb and unveil it. Her heart was beating as she recalled her life as the chosen mother, to her special son. The street made a turn up ahead and she knew the Garden of Gethsemane would suddenly be in sight. As she looked around, she saw the beautiful blue sky. The trees seemed to be greener than usual. Several doves were cooing in the early morning coolness. She felt a great feeling of calmness. What her son had told her about his death had come true, so many unbelievers, and much unrest about his death. Some idolized her son, some whispered, some laughed, but his name was known by everyone.

Today, she could feel him with her as she walked along. After his death, she too asked over and over, "Why my son; why must he die?" The answer had been given to her in the last year.

As she made the last turn, she thought about her feelings of the empty tomb. Her son had risen up from the dead. He had awakened all the disbelievers. He had brought rejoicing to the believers. Her son had given a new meaning to life and to death.

She looked up and the tomb was in front of her, the place that changed so many lives. A warm feeling came over her as she entered removing her sandals.

The tomb was built with a kneeling area, next to the bed, where he had been laid to rest. As she knelt down, she thought about his body, prepared in spices, and then wrapped in a white cloth. Blood still shown in the room. This she knew was from his hands that had been nailed to the cross. She remembered the vigil that took place at the closing of the tomb. A large stone was rolled in front of it, and soldiers standing at attention gazing straight ahead, watching over this sacred place.

Why was she the chosen one to mother over him? She reached into her pocket and felt the cold, smooth and very hard rock. She slowly reached up with the rock and placed it on the edge of the kneeling rail. This meant a year of mourning had come to an end. The tears that only a mother could cry flowed down her cheeks. She whispered softly, "Jesus, dear Jesus, my most holy son."

Suddenly the tears of sadness changed to a feeling of great relief. Her son would always live within her, always be with her, to the end of her life on earth, never to be forgotten.

She heard the footsteps of John entering the holy area. He placed his arms around her and comforted her, in this time of need. He slowly reached in his robe and also added his rock to hers. As Mary turned to go, images of her life flash through her mind.

View of the front and inside of the tomb where Jesus was laid to rest.

MARY'S STORY

CHAPTER 2 A

"Train your child in the way he should go,
and when he is old
he will not turn from it."

Proverbs 22:6

Mary's Life, Birth to 10 Years Old
Possibly September 8, 20 B.C.

As the story might have been told, Mary was born to Joachim and Anne. It was a very warm night and Joachim had taken Anne to the rooftop of their house. An outside wooden ladder took them to the roof. A parapet, required by Jewish law surrounded the edge of the roof. This safeguarded against falling to the ground. It was much cooler on the roof and the beauty of the night sky was all around. Each star was shining brightly and the moon gave a lighted glow over the city and the other rooftops. Joachim had carried up a small wooden cot and a small table with an oil lamp on it. Also, a large bowl filled with water and several cloths were placed near the cot. As he looked into Anne's eyes he could see the look of love. She was not scared and was ready to have this child in her arms.

Earlier Joachim left and brought back Elizabeth, who came from Judah to help with this birth. As she came up to the roof, she could tell by the soft moans from Anne, that the baby was very near. She walked to the cot and whispered to her that she would be by her side to help her. She held her hand and told her to take a deep breath and start gently pushing. She wiped her head with a cool cloth and then told her to do it again. This continued as each time she took a deeper breath, she pushed harder. Elizabeth had much experience with the birth of babies. The woman in the surrounding areas had always requested her, as she knew just how to handle each situation. Suddenly, she saw the head, and told Anne to push once more with all of her might, afterward she could relax. With one last push Elizabeth helped pull the baby out of the canal. It was a girl, what a joy was felt as her voice cried out in the night. The cord was cut and then she wrapped the newborn in swaddling cloth. Joachim took the baby and held it up in the night sky and thanked God for this special blessing. He carried her over to Anne and said, "This is your child named Mary." He placed her in Anne's arms and she snuggled her to her breast. The baby lay content as she bonded to her mother. The picture brought tears to Joachim's eyes as he covered them with a blanket. He quietly cleaned up the area and said goodbye to Elizabeth. What a beautiful evening, and such a blessing to behold. He sat down on the edge of the parapet and looked over at Anne, as she took Mary to her breast for feeding. The evening had such a special feeling as the breeze gently cooled off the hot evening and the stars seemed to be even brighter. He was so happy Elizabeth was there to help him. This would be the start of the special relationship between Elizabeth and Mary. She loved this child from her birth.

The next few days Joachim stayed away from the fields. He wanted to watch over Anne until she could go back to her everyday chores, and still feel well enough to give the added care for this new baby. Anne was a very active woman and Joachim knew that it would give her a lot more responsibility, nursing, cleaning and he thanked God and prayed for the well-being of the child, Mary.

Joachim owned a farm on the outskirts of Nazareth and could hardly wait to get home each day. Such a joy his home was now filled with a child. Mary would become such a special love to him. It was thought that Mary was their only child; it is possible they had another child, which is mentioned in Luke. Her name was given as Salome.

The home that he had built was set on the edge of his farmland. The one large room had an area for cooking and eating. In the center was a large hole that was encircled with large rocks. Firewood was burned in the center. It was used to keep them warm and also to cook food. A large pot hung down over the fire and used to make their meals. All the windows were very high upon the walls. This was to keep out snakes and small animals. The home had a simple table and bench, which Joachim had made. Mats were used to sleep on and during the day they were rolled and put away and then laid out again at night. The home was made out of clay and stone bricks. The walls were covered with a waterproof plaster. The floor was made of hard packed clay bricks laid side by side. The bricks stayed cool in the heat of the summer and warm in the cool winter. Joachim had the home positioned so the cool breezes would blow through the windows in the warm months. He placed it so the outside faced the hillside so they could see the goats and the sheep graze. They could also see the fields and watch the crops grow and ripen for the harvest. This home met all their needs.

Mary's father apparently was a descendant of the great King David, through David's son Nathan. Joachim was proud of his family lineage and carried this with him in his teaching and upbringing of Mary. Mary's mother had ties directly to the clan of Levi, the priests of Israel. Mary's relative Elizabeth was also of Levi descent and the family of Aaron, the first high priest of Israel. Because of the strong religious and priestly influence from both her mother and father, Mary would have grown up with devotion to God and his word. Her mother would have sung her to sleep with the opening words of "Hear, O Israel, and the Lord our God is one Lord." The father of the household recited these words twice every day. Joachim would tell her stories from the Torah, many of these stories were life stories of Mary's people. Many of the events had taken place within a few miles of her front door.

As Mary grew up she would have gone to a synagogue for her education. The schools were free and were supported by the entire community with both contributions and teachings. The Jewish people loved reading the word of God and made sure each child was able to read and write and had knowledge of the scriptures from the great book. The schools had separate classrooms, the boys in one room and the girls in another room. They would all be together at lunch and after school. Much of the education for young girls was conducted from home. Because women married at a young age they had to be capable of managing a household, which was wholly a woman's responsibility. Mary's mother Anne would have taught her the complete running of a household at a very young age, not only baking and cooking, but a very important duty making and mending clothes that the family wore.

The men wore a loincloth around their waists and a shirt under the outerwear. A bright colored over garment with a girdle belt was worn under a cloak, which they could take off or wrap around them when it was cold. Around their heads they wore cloth turbans, which they wrapped around to protect them from the cold winds. They would untie then and let them cover their necks and faces from the hot sun. The women's clothes were very similar, however, the material was finer and the colors were lighter. The under garment was a tunic and it had a longer garment over the top with a belt to hold it together. They had a long panel that was wrapped into the front of the garment. These were used as an apron to wipe their hands as they were working. When the unmarried women went out in public, they wore a veil that showed her modesty. Their clothes changed with the change of seasons. They wore lighter weight fabrics in the warm seasons and heavier in the colder seasons, with the addition of fur and skins to help keep them warm.

On their feet they wore sandals; the soles were made of wood or leather and fastened with straps of leather. They never wore sandals indoors.

The pot that hung over the fire in the center of the house was usually filled and ready to serve family and friends. Usually the pot was filled with a vegetable stew and, on occasion, meat was added. The greatest smell that filled the home was from the fresh bread that was made once a week. Mary's mother taught her well on the proper way to run a household, make clothes, prepare meals, and to give comfort to a family that she would soon be responsible for. Mary was truly happy and very obedient. She grew up with a very religious background, with love of her family and relatives and friends and knowing God is always in control.

Anne holding baby Mary, and Joachim and Cousin Elizabeth at her side

CHAPTER 3 A

"Therefore let us keep the festival
not with the old yeast
the yeast of malice and wickedness,
but with bread without yeast
the bread of sincerity and truth."

1 Corinthians 5:8

Mary From Age 10-13
(Possible spring around 30 B.C.)

Mary looked up at the blue sky as her hair blew in the breeze. Her body went up in the air and then flying back down and back up in the opposite direction. Her best friend and Cousin Elizabeth gave her another push as she flew up higher in the air. The age difference was much different between them. Elizabeth was about 30 to 40 years old; however, they had a great fondness for one another. She seemed to be free as a bird. Her father had made a swing for her by using a long piece of rope hung from a Sycamore tree near the house. Several large knots were tied at the bottom for Mary to place her feet on. Then she held on as Elizabeth pushed her higher and higher. Mary loved to swing. The tree held many memories for Mary. She would spend time by herself sitting in the outspread branches; she would dream about what her future would bring. She jumped off the rope and grabbed Elizabeth and they fell to the ground together in laughter. Elizabeth had come to visit Mary for the early harvest Feast of Wake celebrated during the month that the crops were planted. This spring festival celebrates the completion of the grain seeding. Since Mary's father was a farmer, this was a great tradition in her family, with relatives and friends that lived near Nazareth. It was a time for all to rest after working to plant the fields. Many friends and family that were not farmers would help out in the fields during the early spring. This helped ensure a good harvest. Because God was the center of their lives, it was a time to give thanks and pray for a successful growing season so there would be a successful fall harvest. Elizabeth and her parents came from Judah to take part in this celebration. Her husband Zechariah stayed behind to care for their households.

As Mary and Elizabeth walked away from the swing, they held hands. Mary was so happy to have Elizabeth visiting during this happy, festive time. They loved spending time together, playing and sharing secrets as they walked and sang songs of praise to God. As they came to the edge of town, they found a group of children playing marbles and they stopped and Mary joined in. As the children and Mary played, enjoying each other's company, Elizabeth watched with a great delight as she recalled fond memories from years before when she played the game.

The adults were readying the village for the festival. The women were baking and cooking special foods to be enjoyed together. The men were readying the area where they would all gather together. The women had sewn together cloth to make a tent, which the men put up so they could all eat together outside of the synagogue.

Mary and Elizabeth hear their names being called by Mary's mother. It was time to go in and help get the evening meal ready for their families. They ran down the path to the end of the road that lead them back to Mary's home. They started skipping along and laughing as they returned to help. They could smell the aroma of food in the air. The excitement of the festival made them extremely happy.

They set the table and helped fill the dinner bowls with a warm vegetable soup that their mothers had made. The fresh bread was set around the table for each of the family members to break off pieces as needed. The whole family gathered as they held hands and said a prayer together. The talk at the table was about the festival, which would start the next day.

Mary and Elizabeth pushed their mats together on the floor as they got ready to go to sleep. It was hard for them to settle down and sleep as they knew how much fun they would have in the morning.

As the sun rose over the hillside, Mary's family was already up and joyously finishing the preparations for the festival. Mary was so excited that her mother had made her a new dress. Mary had picked out the light-colored fabric and helped her make the dress. They all gather together and walked to the synagogue.

The day of the feast was one of solemn joy and Thanksgiving that God's protection would watch over and bring a successful completion the activities of the planting season which began several weeks before. It was a day of 'holy convocation.' Work was to cease and the whole community of Israel presented itself before the Lord.

The sheaf, a wrist full of stalks of grain, was presented in a wave offering. The sickle, a curved metal tool used to cut the standing grain, was brought to the altar to represent to God, as the owner of the land and the source of its products. Until its offering, it was unlawful either to begin reaping or to use the new harvest as food. It's offering by the priest was a rite in behalf of all the people, which opened the harvest season. Part of the harvest of the first fruits was put on the altar and the priest consumed the remainder. A male lamb was burned as offering. However, the main significance of the day was the special offering consisting of two loaves of bread.

Elizabeth looked over at Mary; she saw a glowing look on her face. It was now time for the two loaves of bread to be presented. Mary reached over and held her mother's hand. This was a proud day for her family, as Mary's mother had prepared these two beautiful loaves of bread. Mary had helped her mother as she made many loaves so that she could be sure that two loaves would meet the critical test for this special festival. Joachim went to his field and collected the wheat from the new crop. The wheat was then milled and this was given to Anne to bake with leaven. After much comparing the two loaves were picked and then taken to the priest for this special presentation.

Now was the time for the priest to present the loaves of bread and also two lambs as a wave offering on behalf of all the people, because the bread was baked with leaven, they could not be put on the altar; the priest performing the service later then ate them. The priest then invited all males to come to the front of the synagogue and assist with the ceremony by dancing an altar dance during which they sang "Hillel, Praise the Lord". The feast then continued outside of the synagogue. The colorful tent that the women had sewn greeted them, as they started the feast. Everyone in the city was invited. The men had carried tables from their homes and placed them around the outside of the covered area. The women went to their homes and brought food back for eating. The middle was ready for singing, dancing, and spending time with friends, neighbors, and travelling relatives. They gave praise to the Lord and then enjoyed the feast together. This meal was made of many vegetable stews, breads, plates of fresh fruit, and fruitcakes for dessert. The plates of fruit were made up of dates, figs, pomegranates, apples, pears, quince, peaches, and melons. Watermelon and musk melon were the favorites. Honey was sometimes difficult to find, but they used it to dip the fruit in it, when it was available. The vegetable stews were made up of the vegetables grown in the farming area. They used rice, lentils, beans, leeks, garlic, onions, and cucumber to start the stew and then added meats, but only on special occasions such as this. Sheep, game birds, oxen, gazelle, roebuck, and sheep were added to make this stew rich and enough to feed everyone. Of course the bread added richness to the meal. The women all seemed to have learned to make bread in an easy form and baked loaves enough for each week. They also learned how to add fruits to the bread to make special sweet treats for later in the meal. Wine was always served and they always worked together to make enough for the whole year. Grapes were dumped into shallow basins cut from stone. The people of the city took turns stepping on the grapes. The juice was placed into deep vats to ferment into wine. They also dried grapes in the sun to make raisins. Sometimes they put the raisins into cakes. Everyone enjoyed the foods that were prepared. They were proud of each other as they tasted, sipped, and enjoyed each other's company.

Suddenly… everyone stopped and turned toward the sound. Several women began to dance in a circle singing, shaking, and beating cymbals with their hands. Women always began the dancing carrying cymbals made of copper, wound with cestrum, a flowering plant that released a powerful perfume at night. Small objects strung on bars stretched across the frame helped to make lots of noise. Mary reached over and grabbed Elizabeth's hand; they jumped up and joyfully joined in the circle. They giggled and laughed as they circled with all the other girls and women of the town. As they whirled around, the songs they chanted were from the Psalms set to tunes. A group of new men and women slowly grouped together and formed a choir to keep the music alive and directed the singing by rhythm of their clapping of hands.

Many of the men and women, who played instruments, brought them to help with the celebration. The women usually played the lute, a three-stringed triangular instrument. They also liked to play a small harp-like instrument producing a pleasing sound that was called a Lyre. Many of the talented artisans decorated these with silver, Ivory, and many beautiful carvings. Many of the men hand carved long pipes, which they hollowed out and had holes, which they moved their fingers over to make different sounds. The sounds of the singing, clapping, and instruments filled the early evening and kept the dancers holding hands and circling. Singing Psalms, "Praise the Lord, All you nations....all you peoples! For great is his steadfast love toward us and his faithfulness endures forever, Praise the Lord." Everyone was in a fun-filled mood and this continued for several hours. As evening slowly crept across the sky, many children leaned up against their parents' shoulders, eyes growing sleepy. The dancers were circling in a slower pace and everyone was slowing down. The women started clearing the tables and storing the remaining food. The men rounded up the children and helped pick up the area around the tent. It was a time for each person to help pick up and put the area back to the usual order. As the evening stars started showing in the sky the whole town walked back to their homes, carrying tables, food, children, and accessories used for the festival. Their faces showed happiness and serene as they walked along, talking quietly and saying goodbye to friends and relatives. They all knew that by thanking God in this way, the rest of the growing season would be productive and provide them all with the food needed to survive. Mary and Elizabeth were both tired from the full day of celebrating but as they walked along they knew that they must still help light the oil lamps, put down the mats for them all to sleep on, and help Mary's mother, to store the extra food. As they poured water from a pitcher into a bowl to wash up, they both realized that when tomorrow arrived Elizabeth and her parents would have to return to Judah. They would be sad for both Elizabeth and Mary, as cousins, enjoyed the times they spent together. As they lay on the mats, they had placed on the floor; they held hands until they both fell asleep. The happiness of the day was still shown on their faces.

The morning dawn brought the household alive. Elizabeth's family had a long day ahead as they had to travel back to their homes. Mary's mother took a blanket from a shelf and spread it out and laid out in a flat manner their dress clothes. She rolled the blanket up and then in the next layer of the blanket she placed a loaf of bread, dried fruit, and some fresh vegetables and rolled up the rest of the blanket and put a leather strap around it to hold everything they would need for the trip. A cloth strap was put though the rolled blanket and the long ends were knotted together. Elizabeth's father could carry this over his shoulder. A goat skin pouch was filled with water so they would have something to drink on the long trip home.

They enjoyed a breakfast together and then began to say their goodbyes. They hugged each other and wished each other much health and happiness until they saw each other again. They would join a caravan on the edge of town for their journey home.

Mary held Elizabeth in her arms as tears filled her eyes. No girl had meant as much to her as Elizabeth had. The love was seen in the joy of the relationship that they shared.

Elizabeth's family started down the cobblestone street toward the road back to Judah. As they walked along they looked back and waved. Elizabeth turned and walked backward throwing kisses and waving farewell. As they finally disappeared, Mary ran straight to the big sycamore tree. As she climbed the tree, tears fell from her eyes. Her feet pushed up to the highest limb. She leaned up against the trunk and remembered every moment of the days that she and Elizabeth shared together. This was a lonely time for Mary for she knew that in the morning she would have to go back to her everyday life. Joachim and Anne let her spend the rest of the day in the tree. They were glad that Mary had such a close relationship with Elizabeth. She was a good influence in Mary's life.

Each of the next few years repeated one another. Mary studied her religion and was very dedicated. Her parents were very proud of her. She continued to perfect the household skills. She was always a willing worker and everyone in Nazareth knew her and praised her parents for the beautiful woman she was growing into. Even though her parents were poor farm laborers, the love they gave her and the religious training they provided, showed in her confidence and skills she carried with her. She was about to reach her 13th birthday, a time for a woman to be ready to be given to a man in marriage.

Mary and Cousin Elizabeth

CHAPTER 4 A

*"So whenever you eat or drink or whatever
you do do it all for the glory of God."*

1 Corinthians 10:31

Mary At Age 13
(Summer around 32 B.C.)

Mary walked along the cobblestone street, humming and singing praises to her Lord. She was carrying a large basket to put her family's needs in. As she walked past a clay home, with a beautiful wooden door, she caught the eye of Joseph, the carpenter. He was standing in the front of his house, sawing a piece of wood. The sunlight kissed his hair and the muscles in his arms flexed as he worked away. Mary's heart fluttered as she continued down the street. She was on the way to the market to pick up sundries for her mother. The coins clinked in her dress pocket as she strolled along. What was this feeling that played with her heart? She never felt this before.

The carts of fruits and vegetables, spices, cheeses, bakery items, and household needs were in front of her. Many of the women of the town were chatting as they bought the supplies they needed. Mary always liked helping her mother, and she liked taking a stroll to the market and talking with the other women. She stopped and talked to one of her mother's friends. She always felt good when they told her what a beautiful young woman she had grown into. Several other women waved and called a warm greeting to her.

She began picking out the fruits and spices her mother had requested. She carefully checked each melon before picking the perfect one. She grabbed some apples, figs and some dried raisins. Next she went to the spice cart and selected some dill, mint, cumin, and a small container of vinegar. Her father loved spices in their food and on busy days in the field, he loved dipping his bread in vinegar. It was refreshing. Her mother also asked her to get some leeks and garlic to season the vegetable stews. Her mother had a small garden near the wheat field and this helped out with their needs as well.

Mary next turned the corner and found the colorful retail area that sold yards and yards of colorful material. Her mother was a great seamstress and had made several special garments for the owner of the fabric cart. He in return, told her she could get free material. Today he told Mary that he wanted her to pick out several pieces of beautiful material that she liked, because it had been awhile since he paid Mary's mother back with free material.

Colors of material hung from wooden rails overhead. The fabrics waved in the breeze. What a hard time she had in making her choice. The owner was weaving the fabric as he talked with her. He could see the excitement in Mary's face. He wanted her to look at a new fabric design. He had woven golden strands of thread through the colorful stripe of linen fabric. In the sunlight the material twinkled and gave off a rich look. Mary looked at the material, wishing and dreaming of what this would look like on her. The owner broke the silence and said, "How many pieces would you need?" Mary was so shocked she could not speak. He asked, "Is this for you?" She only nodded back. He took a piece of material and held it up to her, then ripped it off in a certain length. She smiled and her face showed a glowing radiance. He nodded to her to follow him down the row of fabrics to the end where the sheer pieces of fabric hung. He selected a very sheer silk piece in a soft gold color that matched the colors of the other material. He looked at her and said, "If you're to have a new dress, you must also have a new veil." Mary's eyes, once again, showed delight. He carefully rolled the sheer material inside the heavier material, and then tied them with a long piece of material. He handed her the material, and told her to enjoy her new outfit.

Mary took the material and carefully placed it over the fruits and vegetables in the basket. She waved goodbye and turned to complete her errands. She now had one thing left to do. Her mother gave her instructions to go to the fish market and see if the fishermen had come in with a fresh catch. As she made the turn, she could see many people gathered around the fish cart. Because it was a warm day, her mother told her to go there last so the fish would stay fresh.

The fish were laid out in the shade of the cart and cool water was poured over them every few minutes. Mary did not know the kinds of fish, but knew this was a very rare occurrence for her family to purchase fish, so she knew she must make a wise selection. She found the fish and asked the fisherman to wrap it for her. He took large leaves from a tree and wrapped it up and in return for a few coins; she took the fish and put it deep in the basket. Now it was time to return home as fast as she could.

She retraced the street on which she had come. Her parents lived on the outskirts of Nazareth as farmers lived close to their fields, but within the safety of the town. Once again, she passed by the home of Joseph. He saw her coming and waved to her and called out, "How are you Mary?" She felt his eyes on hers and suddenly this strange feeling came over her again. "I'm fine, Joseph, however, I must return home as I have fish for our evening meal." He smiled and waved again to her.

Her mother was waiting at the front door and helped her put the basket on the table. Mary could smell the fresh bread. She knew this would be a great meal but also felt that something unstated was out of the ordinary. Her mother was delighted with the selection of material and was surprised that the owner had given her such a beautiful piece of golden silk. Anne smiled as she put the material on the shelf. She would start this special dress in the morning.

Mary helped her mother prepare the evening meal. The fresh bread was put on the table surrounded by fresh fruit. The fish was prepared on a board that was put over the fire, seasoned with dill and garlic. The home was filled with a wonderful smell. Joachim walked through the front door and smiled with delight. Mary prepared a large basin of water and washed her father's feet. She knew he had a hard day in the field and she knew this cooled him. She gave him a glass of wine to quench his thirst.

The table was ready and Mary remembered the vinegar that her father liked to dip his bread in. Mary's mother brought out the biggest oil lamp they had. Mary suddenly felt that something big was going to happen. Her father and mother took their places. Mary sat between them. They held hands and said the prayer for the meal. The meal was delicious and Mary felt proud to have such loving parents.

After dinner her father asked her to stay at the table. They wanted to speak to her. Her father told her that he and her mother were very proud of the way she had taken over the responsibility of the household and her religious learning. It was now time for her to take a husband, and begin her own life. Since it was customary for her marriage to be arranged, her father explained that he and her mother had spent much time selecting this man. Because they wanted the very best for her, they had selected a very religious man, and an ambitious man. His name was Joseph, the town's best carpenter. Mary gasped with censured delight. A husband and it was to be Joseph, the carpenter. She suddenly felt an uncertain feeling. Leave her mother and father. Marry a man and become a wife.

Her father then told her that in two weeks they would announce this at the synagogue in a special service. She would meet Joseph at that time.

This night was to be a sleepless one. What would it be like leaving home? What would it be like living with someone she didn't even know? What if they didn't like each other? What if she couldn't please him? But he seemed so nice, and he did make her feel different. "Oh dear Lord, please watch over me."

The next two weeks seemed to pass very quickly. Her mother Anne was busy sewing a new dress. The colorful material Mary had picked in the market weeks ago was flowing into a beautiful dress. The gold silk scarf was formed into a beautiful gold veil. Mary spent many days standing on a small stool as her mother stitched each seam and she helped hold the material straight to complete the dress, just as she dreamt it. These days were filled with talk of her new role as wife. Her mother reassured her of her husband to be. The finishing was the veil, which wound around her head, back around her neck and over her lower face. The gold color highlighted her and gave her an angelic look. Her mother beamed with love. Her father looked at his little girl with tears in his eyes. Their lives were about to begin to change.

The early Sabbath morning was filled with sounds. A mourning dove cooed in the distance and a soft breeze pushed through the leaves on Mary's favorite Sycamore tree. They were up early to get ready for this blessed day. Mary's mother fixed a light meal of fresh fruit, bread, cheese, and some sliced melon and apples. They had fresh goats milk and some cool water from the well. As Mary finished eating, her mother combed through her hair and wound it up and put two crossed wooden carved spikes to hold it up. She already had her under tunic on and her mother helped her slip on her beautiful new dress on top. Then the gold veil was wound around her head. Her mother went to a shelf and took a bone coiled bracelet, with a serpent head carved on each end. She slipped this on Mary's arm. Mary knew how special this bracelet was to her mother. Her mother kissed her lightly on the cheek and they went to the front door where Joachim was waiting. They all slipped on their sandals and as they stepped out the front door. Joachim put his arm around Mary, and they began walking toward the synagogue.

The Sabbath service was as usual, with high priest conducting the service. Because the temple that was in their town was smaller, they did not have a high priest. The priest that was in charge of this clan was well known and dressed in ordinary garb. His robe was very simple and he wore a sash, which was decorated, to his rank. The most important task was to teach his people the "Law of God". His clan provided his means to live. A part of all their harvests and livestock were given to him for his working for God. When the Sabbath was not revolving around a festival or holy days, the service was of worship and studying God's law, as it would be this day.

As Joachim, Anne, and Mary enter the tabernacle, Mary and Anne went to the side where the women were seated. Joachim went to the other side where Joseph was already seated. The service started with singing of several Psalms and scripture read from the holy Torah. The priest then spoke to his clan on what the laws of God meant to his people.

Mary kept looking across the aisle at Joseph. He was dressed in a beautiful beige woven linen robe. He wore a leather belt that secured his outer garment to his under tunic. His hair washed clean, shined in the light. His face had a gentle look. He looked over at Mary and gave her a smile. Mary quickly looked away as she felt her face redden. Mary did not hear the service as her mind wondered on what her new life would be like. Her heart beat faster as she heard the priest call her name and her mother and father's names. They all walked forward to the front of the synagogue where the priest stood to give the blessing. The priest then called Joseph to come forward. Joseph slowly rose to making his way forward with confidence and assurance. He stopped at Mary's side. The priest took Mary's hand, and then took Joseph's hand, and placed them in one another's. Mary felt this a comforting moment. She looked up at him and his eyes were filled with love. The priest then announced to the clan that the arrangement of the marriage was to be prepared in the eyes of God. This would take a year and that at the end of that time, the wedding would be held. He asked the clan to pray with him for God to watch over them.

After the service, the many friends and relatives congregated around Mary and Joseph. Everyone was happy about the forthcoming marriage of the two.

It is believed that possibly Joseph had been married before and that his wife had died. Also, it could be possible that Joseph had several grown children that might have been at the service.

As they stood together in front of the synagogue, suddenly a hand reached over to Mary. Mary gasped with joy. It was Elizabeth. She grabbed her and tears came out of her eyes. The excitement of the day had overcome her. They talked together and then Elizabeth whispered in Mary's ear "I'm so happy for you." Everyone felt the love between them. This was a day of happiness for both of them. Several more hugs were shared.

Several friends came forward and announced that they wanted Mary's family, Joseph, Elizabeth and her husband to come to their homes for lunch. They all walked along chatting and talking about the special occasion that would take place in the next year.

The happiness continued throughout the meal, and Joseph seemed to fit into the family. Joachim and Anne had made an excellent choice for Mary. Everyone felt it as plans were started for the marriage.

The day seemed to go too fast, and soon it was time for Elizabeth and her husband, Zechariah to leave, to go back to Judah. Good-byes were said, and a promise by Mary to come and see her, as she would not be travelling for a while.

Then Joseph had to leave and Mary's mother had invited him to come to lunch on the next weekend. Joseph took Mary's hand; he gave it a kiss and said he looked forward to seeing them all next weekend. As Joachim, Anne, and Mary walked home, content that this Sabbath day had been very special. In one year Mary and Joseph would become one, and start a new life.

Mary at the market

CHAPTER 5 A

"Trust in the Lord with all your heart and
lean not on your own understanding. In all
ways acknowledge him
and he will make your paths straight."

Proverbs 3:5-6

Several Months Later

As Mary walked along, she sang a favorite Psalm of praise to the Lord as she was going to one of her favorite places. This place was away from the town of Nazareth. As she walked down the road, she could see the water in the distance. There was a special place on a rocky hillside that she loved to go to for peace and contentment. A cave that she knew about was just ahead of her. She pulled up her toga dress and pulled herself up onto the cave entrance and then looked out over the water. The water went on forever. The waves slowly came up to the shore and about every seventh wave made a louder crash on the shore. The peacefulness was everywhere. She was alone with herself feeling pleasures of the water and the blue sky and the calmness of the air around her.

Suddenly, a bright light appeared and scared her. Out of the immense light and angel appeared. This was the angel Gabriel. The words of this angel were very clear to Mary, "Greetings, you who are highly favored! The Lord is with you." Mary looked up with a startled look. The beauty of this angel mesmerized Mary. Gabriel added, "Mary, do not be afraid. You have found favor with God." Mary was greatly troubled and she responded with "Why me?" I have nothing good in myself to offer. God, why would he choose me? Gabriel reassured her, "Do not be afraid, Mary." "You will be with child and give birth to a son, and you are to give him the name Jesus. He will be great and will be called the son of the Most High. The Lord God will give him the throne of his father David, and he will reign over the house of Jacob forever; his kingdom will never end."

Mary sat silently, and then looked up at Gabriel with a question, "How will this be? I am a virgin?" The angel responded in a very strong and powerful voice. "The Holy Spirit will come upon you and the power of the Most High will overshadow you. So the holy one to be born, will be called the Son of God." Mary was in total confusion, and showed this in her face. Then Gabriel told Mary about her cousin Elizabeth, a woman that was no more than sixty years old, who was unable to bear children, but who now was about six months pregnant. Mary was in disbelief! Elizabeth was with child? That was impossible, she is to old. They had spent many hours talking about why she was unable to conceive. How could this be, she was now an older woman. Then Gabriel added a promise to her, "For nothing is impossible with God." Then a discussion was carried on about trust in God, and this was a privilege that no other woman would have. God had chosen her as a vessel through which God's son would become human. Mary heard her voice speak up in the quiet silence of the day. "I am the Lord's servant. May it be me as you have said?" As suddenly as the angel Gabriel had appeared, the angel had disappeared. The brightness of the light was gone. Mary was alone. Her mind was very confused. What had she just said? She loved her Lord, but how could she be chosen? She had just accepted this challenge.

She went home and carefully told her mother and father. They were unbelieving that their daughter could be pregnant. Suddenly, she wanted to see Elizabeth and share her joy. She begged her parents to allow her to visit Elizabeth to see if what she had heard was true. They told her they would let her go if she joined a caravan. The road that leads to Elizabeth and Zechariah's home had several caravans each day, and it would be easy for Mary to leave and later come back. Also her parents would know if she got there safe, and it would allow messages to be sent back and forth. It would be about 69 miles and take her about four to five days. Mary always liked to travel with the caravans, they had plenty of food and water and she liked meeting the other travelers. It was a very safe way to travel.

Her father came from the back of the house with a donkey that would make the trip easier. Her mother brought some food and a goat skin pouch filled with water. She tied them at the front of the donkey wound up in a blanket. Mary led the donkey down the road to meet up with the caravan. She made the last turn and spun around and waved good bye to her parents. The road was ahead and her journey began. She hurried as fast as she could, as she couldn't wait to see Elizabeth. Several days later she saw the hillsides of Judah in front of her. She knew the road that led to Elizabeth's house was near. She left the caravan and she and the donkey climbed the hillside to the path that lead to her house. She called out Elizabeth's name, and suddenly she appeared at the front of the house. She ran to greet her. When Elizabeth heard Mary's greeting, the baby leaped in her womb and Elizabeth was filled with the Holy Spirit. In a loud voice she exclaimed, "Blessed are you among women and blessed is the child you will bear!" "But why am I so favored that the mother of my lord should come to me?" As soon as the sound of your greeting reached my ears, the baby in my womb leapt for joy. Blessed is she who believed that what the Lord said to her will be accomplished!" Then Mary burst into song,

"My soul glorifies the Lord.
And my spirit rejoices in God my savior.
For he has been mindful
of the humble state of his servant.
From now on all generations will call me blessed,
the mighty one has done great things for me
Holy is his name.
His mercy extends to those who fear him,
From generation to generation
He has performed mighty deeds with his arm.
He has scattered those who are proud in their inmost thoughts.
He has brought down rulers from their thrones
but has filled the humble.
He has filled the hungry with good things.
But has sent the rich away empty.
He has helped his servant Israel,
Remembering to be merciful
To Abraham and his descendants
Forever, even as he said to our fathers." (Luke 1:46-55)

When Mary ended this beautiful song (later to be known as Mary's song), they held each other as tears filled their eyes. What a joy, both having wombs filled with child, both carrying children who would grow into men that would take a place in the future of all people. Elizabeth would give birth to John the Baptist and Mary would give birth to the Messiah, Jesus Christ.

Mary spent the next three months with Elizabeth and Zechariah. Elizabeth was between 6 and 7 months pregnant while Mary was only several months with child. The difference in their ages did not take away from the joy they both felt. The days and nights were filled with talk of the babies that would soon be born. Mary helped Elizabeth with her household duties and together they cooked and sewed clothes for themselves and the babies. Mary was so glad to have Elizabeth to talk with about what other people would think about her situation. An unwed woman with child could cause a lot of talk and what would her husband-to-be think about this? Elizabeth understood the Lord's plan and together they rejoiced in each other. This strength gave Mary more faith in her future.

It was soon time for Mary to leave and go back to her parent's home. Zechariah had prepared her donkey and Elizabeth insisted that Mary take some fresh vegetables, fruit, and bread with her to eat along the way home. The baby clothes were wrapped in a blanket. It was the summer of their calendar year, and it would be a long, hot trip back to Nazareth. A goatskin pouch filled with fresh water would help quench her thirst. The donkey seemed to know where he was going, home. Zechariah helped Mary up on the donkey and as she sat sideways on the back of the animal, Elizabeth held her hand and the donkey slowly started down the dusty road. Elizabeth and Zechariah walked along with Mary and the donkey. Both Elizabeth and Mary knew it would be a long time before they would see each other again. The road took a sharp turn as the donkey continued forward to join up with the caravan. Elizabeth and Zechariah stopped and waved good-bye. Mary turned and waved back. Then they both disappeared, and Mary felt the solitude of the trip home. She placed her hand on her swelling stomach and realized she wasn't alone. A warm feeling came over her. Having been with Elizabeth had given her a sense of the child growing inside her as the day went by. The hours on the donkey didn't seem to bother her and she drank the fresh water and ate several pieces of fruit as the donkey kept the pace on the road with the other animals in the caravan. The days went fast. Soon Mary could see the town of Nazareth. The farm houses on the outskirts framed against the hillside. The farm animals were heard as they were bleating and bahhing in the summer air. Bells ringing on goats filled the country side with a familiar sound. Mary was happy to be coming back home. As the donkey wound around the hillside, the main road to town was ahead. Several people from the town were also walking along the road. They looked at her in a strange way. Mary seemed unaware as she entered the town. The sounds of the town started filling the air. Since her parents' house was on the outskirts, she was almost home. The donkey made the turn as they left the caravan. Several of the women that she knew from the market stopped and looked at her. She realized they were looking at her swollen stomach. They put their heads down and started chattering between themselves. Mary felt a strange feeling, as she knew they were talking about her. One of them called out, "Where have you been?" Mary called back, "In Judah, with Elizabeth." They all seemed to chuckle and continued on.

She saw her parents' home ahead and her mom and dad were standing out in front. The donkey went right up to the front door. Joachim took Mary's hand and helped her off the donkey. He took the donkey away to give it a drink of water. Anne took Mary into the house and gave her a warm meal. The evening conversation was about Elizabeth and the two babies that would be born. It was evident to her parents that she was with child. They still didn't completely understand, but Mary was their daughter and they would protect her.

Mary's mother told her that Joseph had come over many time to find out when she would be back and she should go and see him tomorrow. After the long trip Mary was exhausted as she lay down on her mat, she thanked God for her time with Elizabeth and for the safe trip back home.

The next morning Mary told her mother that she would go to the market for her. As she walked down the cobblestone street, she felt people passing her and looking at her stomach. She could not hide it. The looks were of disbelief. Who was this lovely girl with? Who was the father? Why had she left for such a long period of time? As she walked past Joseph's home, he was in the yard working. He looked up and waved at Mary. He called to her; "I'll see you tonight!" She once again felt the flutter in her heart. This was her Joseph, that man that she would marry. He was one of the only people that day that didn't look at her in a strange way. She finished the marketing and went back to her home and helped her mother with the household chores. Mary was glad to be back and feeling confident about her baby and her new life. Joachim had invited Joseph for dinner so he and Mary could spend the evening together. Also planning had to be finished for their marriage.

The knock on the door gave Mary a stir, this would be Joseph. She walked to the door and opened it. Joseph looked at her with a disappointing look. Her stomach showed through her tunic dress. He looked at her with an astonished and shocked look. "Mary, are you with child?" She looked at him with a pride in her eyes, "Joseph, the Lord has blessed us!" "Mary, how could you say that? I'm not the father! Whom have you been with?"

She smiled back and said, "This baby is given to us by our God." The angel Gabriel came to me and told me I was the chosen woman to give birth to this child, this child to be named Jesus. This child is the promised deliverer, the Messiah, God's son.

Joseph looked over at Mary's parents and hung his head. He turned and left before the evening meal. Silence fell over the room. They ate the meal and only spoke of what Mary would do. A woman in this day before the restriction of Roman law, an adulteress, would be stoned. This was adultery even though the marriage was not consummated. The Jewish custom of betrothal period was the exchange of a solemn vow, as binding as a modern wedding. Mary's parents loved Mary and told her they would help her. They could see in her face the confidence that was given her by her faith. This child, they were convinced, was from God.

Joseph had left and went back to his home. His only thoughts were on what an embarrassment Mary had caused him. His only option was a private divorce. The custom was to have two or three trusted friends stand up and be witnesses. Joseph would then present Mary with a bill of divorce. He did not have to give a reason. This could be done very privately and in just a day or two. He would go on with his life alone, and Mary would be left with her family and the humiliation of child bearing and raising the child alone. It would be very possible that she would be stoned and an outcast in this town. His mind was exhausted with thoughts of what he should do. He knew in his mind that he still loved Mary. As he rested, a feeling of trust in God came over him. As he slept, an angel spoke to him and told him that Mary was telling the truth. She was carrying the Messiah in her womb. She had not been unfaithful and the child was God himself of human flesh. "Do not be afraid to take Mary home as your wife. What is conceived in her is from the Holy Spirit. She will give birth to a son and you are to give him the name Jesus. He will save his people from their sins." Joseph lay awake for many hours thinking about what the angel had said, "A son, Jesus, to save us from sin." This is what Mary had said. It must be true. He was a righteous man and he must obey God. The sun soon came up and he knew he must go back and see Mary. He must put his trust and faith in God.

Mary was reading from the Torah when she heard a knock on the door. She went slowly to the door and opened it. There stood Joseph.

The morning light surrounded him. He looked at Mary and then asked her to come with him to the courtyard. They walked together down the cobblestone path and found an area where they could sit together. Joseph reached over and took Mary's hand. He then spoke and said, "An angel also came to me and told me you were speaking the truth yesterday." This will be a special baby and please, please Mary if you will still have me, I want to marry you and help you raise this child as my own.

Mary was overwhelmed with a great feeling of love and security. She looked up at Joseph and tears fell from her eyes. "Oh, Joseph, my dear Joseph! I promise to give you a life filled with love and the glory of God."

Mary and Joseph sat for a long time getting to know each other. Talking and feeling the joy of the Lord overtake them; they knew that together their lives would be filled with a great deal of love. They knew that they were meant for each other.

They walked together back to Mary's home. As they entered the front room, Mary's mother stopped and turned to look at them. She could see the look in their eyes and knew that their future together had been reaffirmed.

Steps were heard on the front cobblestones. The door opened up and Joachim entered his home. He too saw the look in Mary and Joseph's faces. This was a very happy day for Mary's parents. Joachim said a special blessing to the happy couple. They ate lunch together and made plans for the upcoming marriage. Because of the baby that would be born in about 5 months, they all decided that marrying sooner than the one-year betrothal should take place. Happiness filled the air and Anne and Joachim were especially happy, as they knew that Joseph would take good care of Mary and that their household would be filled with the love of God.

The days were filled with plans for the special day, food, music, and the invitation of friends was all to be prepared.

Mary and Angel Gabriel

CHAPTER 6 A

"Husbands, love your wives. Just as Christ
loved the church and gave himself up
for her."

Ephesians 5:25

Mary and Joseph's Wedding

The day dawned with a beautiful sunrise. Mary arose and went to the front of her home and watched the blaze of color come up over the hillside. She kneeled down and praised the Lord for the joy he had given her. The quietness of the morning was all around her. This was the day that would change her whole life. She would leave this home that she had lived in all her life and tonight she would start her new life in another man's home. She reached down and felt the life growing inside her. She knew she was taking a life with her. She walked down the path to a stream of water that flowed through her father's land, from the Jordan River. She found a quiet area in the water and then looked at the image of her face. She felt her face with her hands. She took off her dress and went into the water and cleaned her body. The water was cool and refreshing. She washed her hair and let it hang loose to dry. She came back and sat quietly in the morning sun. She heard her mother and father stirring in the house. Her mother called to her to come and have something to eat. As they sat together, her father gave the morning blessing. He looked into her eyes and asked the Lord to give her peace and love and a day filled with the love of the Lord. He read from the Torah and they gave thanks together. As they enjoyed the morning lunch together, they all felt the changes that would take place in their lives. Mary would walk out of the door and into another life while Anne and Joachim would stay behind in their home and feel the loss of their child.

Anne and Mary together had made the plans for this day. A special dress had been made. They both always enjoyed sewing together and they designed a dress that covered her stomach in such a way that people would not criticize her pregnancy. The cloth was made of flax plant and they made it into a very fine material. They attached the flax to a stick called a distaff and twisted the fiber into thread, and then the thread was woven into cloth. The lengthwise thread was attached to a wooden beam on the loom; the finer the thread the lighter the material.

Everyone in the town was invited to the wedding; however, this wedding was different. Many of the people in the town were upset with the marriage of Mary and Joseph. Many of the people made it known through gossip that they would not attend. Anne was not going to let this gossip and the lack of people attendance spoil her daughter's wedding. She enjoyed the last few days having special time alone with Mary. She knew that Mary had been taught the ways of a woman that would give her the ability to raise a family with the surrounding love of the Lord.

After lunch Mary went to her small room and packed her few personal belongings. She carefully rolled her clothes into mats and woven blankets. Her mother brought in some household items that she thought Mary would need. Everything was carefully packed and arranged for her departure. Now it was time to dress and arrange her hair. As she slipped into her light-colored flowing dress, she felt the roundness of her stomach. She would be carrying this special blessing with her on her wedding day. She took her comb and brushed out her hair. She took the long cream colored silk scarf that she and her mother had picked out. She wound it around her head and twisted it around her neck. The extra length fell down on each side of the front of her dress.

They had made perfume by mixing frankincense, myrrh, and aloe. Anne wanted Mary to have special scents to take with her. Mary took henna and rubbed it on her lips to stain them red for the day. She heard footsteps coming to her little room. She turned around and there stood her mother and father. Tears fell from her mother's eyes and Mary could see the pride in her father's too. He was holding a brand new pair of sandals, which he held out to her. He had worked especially hard to be able to buy these leather sandals for her wedding. Since sandals were never put on in the house they all walked to the front door. Joachim bent down and carefully placed them in front of Mary. Mary slipped into them and he tied the leather straps around her ankles. His little girl was now all grown up. The late afternoon sun was hanging low in the sky. It was time for them to go to the synagogue. They walked down the path to the cobblestone roadway that led to the special temple. Mary walked in the middle with her parents on each side. Joachim was dressed in his best robe and a new turban wrapped around his head. He carried a wooden staff. He walked along with his arm around Mary. Anne was wearing a soft, light-colored striped toga. A soft colored scarf wrapped around her head. She held Mary's hand. Her face showed the lines of age and her eyes showed the look of impending loneliness.

They walked along and nodded and spoke to friends and neighbors. Anne hoped that Mary would not feel hurt because they could see that many townsfolk were not going. They walked along slowly, as they all wanted to be together for as long as possible. They walked along with other friends that were joining them for the ceremony. As they entered this holy place, they went to the front to be seated. Anne had placed fresh flowers on the altar and friends and relatives had brought small gifts of food and household items. They were placed among the flowers and gave the front of the altar area a very special look.

Usually the men sat on one side of the synagogue and the women on the other. Today was different. They would sit together. This was a uniting of the two people and a time to celebrate the beginning of their lives together. The few town's people and relatives enter the synagogue and took seats. Mary's mother left for a few minutes to make sure the food in the back of the church was ready for a simple dinner that they would share together.

Sounds came from the back of the church. Joseph and many of his friends and family came into the synagogue. He walked down the aisle with great confidence. He looked over at Mary and gave her a smile that gave her a sense of joy. He sat in the front row and his friends and family seated themselves around him. The synagogue had a quiet sound of hushed voices as many of the people were carrying on a quiet conversation about the couple, the weather, and happenings that had taken place in the town of Galilee.

After a few minutes, the priest entered at the front of the altar. He was wearing a white robe, since he was not a high priest. However, the sash he wore was colorful and showed in the decoration of it, that he was of a high rank. A hush came over the synagogue. The service started with a song of blessing sung by the body of people attending. The priest put his hand out and invited Mary and Joseph to come forward to the front of the altar. He took both of their hands and gave a blessing to the both of them. He read scriptures from the Torah. Joseph looked over at Mary and saw the beauty in her eyes and felt the love around them. The priest then wound a beautiful embroidered scarf around their hands. This was a symbol of the binding of their two lives. The priest then called Joachim up to the altar as it was time for him to receive the Mohar, a fee paid by Joseph. Since Mary was considered a working asset, Joseph had to pay Joachim for her. In return Joachim then gave Joseph and Mary a dowry. This consisted of a list of things that they would receive from his household. This was not a large dowry as Joachim and Anne were not wealthy people. Mary had tears in her eyes as she learned that the donkey that carried her to Elizabeth's house was to be given to them. Also seedlings from the many crops he grew were to be given to them to start a garden. Mary and Joseph then received the blessing of the union of marriage. The people stood and sang and rejoiced to this marriage. They all followed Mary and Joseph to the back of the synagogue. It was now time to eat and drink to the congratulations that were given to the happy couple. Joachim and Anne were so filled with joy at last Mary was going forward with her life and they would not have to worry so much about her and the baby. They had taken Joseph into their family, as one of them, and trusted him to take care of their beloved Mary.

After much toasting to the couple, and much eating, it was time to finish the ceremony. It was customary for Mary to go back to her parent's home. She stayed dressed in her wedding dress. After dark the bridegroom and his party went in the procession to the bride's home to reclaim his new wife. A blessing was once again given to the couple. Joachim had the donkey waiting and Joseph put her on her donkey and then together they went through the village to his home. As the donkey walked along carrying the precious Mary, Joseph looked at her in awe. This was his new wife and he would soon be blessed with a child. It was a custom for the friends and relatives to follow behind carrying lit torches. The lighted procession could be seen through the town and even shepherds on the hillside watched the parade of lights. People in the town who had not gone to the wedding came to their door-ways to watch the couple. Many of them shook their heads in disgust.

After the long walk Mary, Joseph, and the donkey were in front of Joseph's house. The same house she had passed so many times before going to and from the market. Today, this house became her new home. The townsfolk and friends cheered for the new couple as they delivered them to their home, wishing them health and happiness before departing themselves. Mary got off the donkey and Joseph tied him to a tree in the front courtyard. Joseph put his arm around Mary and they walked to the front door. Once there, they turned and waved to the crowd. Joseph unlocked the front door, took Mary's things, and together they entered their home.

Mary and Joseph's wedding ceremony

CHAPTER 7 A

*"Come to me, all you who are weary and burdened
and I will give you rest."*

Mathew 11:28

3 Months Later

Mary knew something was wrong. In the last few months she had learned the ways of her new husband. The last few nights in front of the lamp light, Joseph had held his head in his hands. His face showed a great concern. Mary was taught never to push a man for expressing his concerns. She knew with time he would confide in her.

Since the day of their marriage, Mary put the household together. The home that Joseph had was much finer than the one of her parents. The table and chairs were of fine wood. She could tell that Joseph had spent several weeks before their marriage getting ready for her. This house was in the center of town. As you passed through the front door, you entered a porch furnished with seats and a bench. Several skin mats were placed on the hardened mud floor. Straw mats at the entrance were laid down, where their sandals would be put. A low bench held a terra cotta bowl with a ladle for quenching your thirst upon entering the house. From this room stairs lead down to the main rooms. The room for cooking was in the lower area. This was very pleasant for Mary as she loved to bake and cook and it stayed cooler in this area. A large table was in the middle of the room and several chairs were arranged around it. An oven was built into the wall with a ledge built over the flames. An overhead hook held the pots for cooking the meals. And a ledge built higher on the wall was used for storing flour and baking items. It was easy to see that this was Mary's favorite room. Dried herbs hung around the room and terra cotta earthenware's were arranged around the area. They were filled with olive oil, fruits and vegetables. On the wall, pegs hung 'craters', large containers used to bathe feet. Off of this room were bedrooms, one on each side. These were modest rooms with a simple mat on each floor and a small bench with several small clay oil lamps. These were left burning all night for security. In this home the lamp was a symbol of the life and dignity of this Jewish family.

Mary was very happy in this house, even if it was very hot and stuffy in warm months and cold and damp in the cold months. She took over her role with grace and ease.

As she looked up from her kneading of bread, she saw the look in Joseph's eyes. He sat at the other end of the table. He spoke to her in a concerned voice, "Mary, Cesar Augustus has sent out a decree that a census should be taken of the entire Roman world. Because I belong to the house and line of David, I must register in Bethlehem." This is about eighty miles from here and will take me four or five days. My dear Mary, this comes at a very bad time in your pregnancy. I will have to leave you behind. How can I do this?" His head sank. "God, please help me at this time! Why must I do this?" Silence was felt in the room. Mary wondered how she could stay behind, alone, leaving her husband to travel alone and worry about her. "Joseph, my dear, I cannot be left alone here without you. I do not want to stay behind." Please give me a day or two to prepare for this trip and we shall make it together." Joseph's head came up and his eyes caught hers. "Mary, my dear Mary, you cannot make this trip. You are very pregnant and due to deliver any day now, certainly I cannot take you!" Mary turned and walked around the table to where Joseph sat. She placed her hand on his shoulder and spoke in a very confident voice, "I will not stay behind. I am strong and we will be together when our blessed baby is born. Now let us go and prepare for this trip. There is too much to be done to deliberate any further about my going or not. I'm going with you!"

The next two days went very quickly. Mary went to the outside of town and told her parents of her plans. They were upset but understood that as a woman her duty was to accompany her husband. Her mother gave her some fruits and vegetables and a warm blanket that she had just finished weaving. They could use it on the ground as a bed and it was so large they could pull the extra length over them to keep them warm. She kissed them both and said her farewell. Her mother walked with her back to the house and helped carry all these items. As they entered the house, Joseph was there to greet them. He told Anne he was worried about Mary on this trip. Mary turned and looked at both of them, "Please don't worry, we have our Lord to guide us and we have each other for strength and trust. Mother, come and help me prepare this house for closing until we return." Her mother told them that she would daily check on the house.

The morning was cloudy and cool. Joseph brought the donkey out in front. He hung goatskin water containers, a canvas pouch filled with two loaves of freshly baked flat bread, fruit and vegetables, some fig cakes. Joseph knew the meals would be filled with fish as they would be traveling along the Jordan River. Mary walked out of the house carrying the blanket, rolled carefully into a small pack. Joseph tied this onto the goatskin containers. Everything was tied near the front of the donkey so there was more room for Mary to ride.

Joseph was dressed in a tunic with heavy wrap hanging loosely around him. He knew the evenings would be cool and the wrap would give him added warmth. He made sure Mary also had a heavy wrap over her tunic. She wore a heavy head wrap that she could wrap around her neck for warmth. They both wore heavier type sandals to keep their feet warm.

Joseph stepped forward and placed the large key in the front door. It was time to lock the house and begin the journey. The key clicked and Joseph tested the knob to make sure it was secure. He then tied the large key to a cord around his waist and dropped into an inside pocket. He wanted to make sure this key was attached to his body. This was his home and it was his asset for the future.

It was very early in the morning and the only sound around was the cooing of the mourning doves. The town was still at peace and the only people stirring were Mary and Joseph. They untied the donkey and walked out of the entryway of their home. The donkey's hoofs clip-clopped on the cobblestone street and along with this sound, Mary and Joseph's sandals scuffed along the street. As they walked along, they looked at each other. They both knew this would be a long journey. As they rounded a bend, they both stopped and looked back at their home. They knew they would miss the home life they had enjoyed together but they must continue on; the road before them narrowed as they came to the edge of Nazareth. The well was in front of them. Joseph had planned that the last stop would be to fill the two goatskin water pouches. He dropped the water pail down into the well and heard the splash. Mary watched as he pulled the pail back up. He filled the pouches and then hung them back over the donkey's neck. Next he filled the pail again and he and Mary drank the cold, refreshing water. The last pail pulled up was for the donkey. He lapped at the water and it was as if this animal knew that this was to be a long trip. It took time for him to get filled up. Mary and Joseph sat on the edge of the well. Joseph took Mary's hand and together they prayed to the Lord, to watch over them and give them a safe trip. Joseph picked up his staff and this meant the journey was to begin. Together the three walked down to road toward the last turn. They knew this would lead them to the Jordan River. Once at the river they would turn south and follow the river bank to Bethlehem.

Joseph had carefully planned the trip and knew the next four to five days would be of great concern. The weather, wild animals, the threat of rebels and of course Mary's pregnancy. As the terrain became rougher and the trees and scrubs thickened nearer the road, Joseph looked over at Mary. A glow was showing on her face. Her stomach had enlarged and she could not conceal the full term belly. She seemed filled with a serene Holy grace. She looked over at him and with a happy and joyous smile. It gave Joseph a great feeling of love and he felt a confidence he had never felt before.

Joseph knew that the early mornings would be the time to make up most of the walking, if they got behind. They would stop at the middle of the day when it was hottest and then continue on until darkness overcame them. This would be the easiest on Mary. She would ride the donkey when she grew tired.

Because they were still close to Nazareth, the road they were on had many other people traveling so they were not alone. The first day went very quickly. When the sun was high in the sky, they stopped for a rest and to eat. They found a large Sycamore tree with spreading branches that provided a good deal of shade. Joseph took the food from the donkey and let the animal go to the river to get a drink and to graze on the edge of the bank. Mary spread out the blanket and they both drank some water and they broke off pieces of flat bread. They ate slowly as they leaned up against the large tree trunk. It was still cool and an overcast day and they appreciated the breeze blowing through the leaves. Mary rubbed her stomach and felt the movement inside. She knew that the birth was close.

After they finished eating, Joseph brought the donkey up to the tree and tied him to one of the lower limbs. Then he and Mary leaned back and took a nap. They both knew this sleep was needed so they could continue on until dark.

After about an hour and a half, Joseph stirred and looked around. The donkey had lain down and Joseph went over and rubbed his head. He untied the donkey and quietly took him back down to the water so he could be filled again with water. Joseph took off his robe and walked out into the water to have a river bath. The water flowed by and the coolness gave a refreshing jolt to his body. He put his head under the water to wet his hair. He stood for a few minutes and looked at the mountains and the green foliage around him. He heard a noise behind him as Mary was now wading in too. She took a handful of water and threw it at him. He splashed her back. They laughed at each other and then Mary splashed some cool water on her face and arms to freshen herself. Together, with the donkey, they walked back to the blanket and put their sandals on. They rolled the blanket back up and Joseph picked up his staff. This, once again, meant it was time to continue on. Being refreshed gave them a chance to walk faster for a few miles. Joseph knew it was important to walk at least 20 miles each day in order to get to Bethlehem in four to five days. He estimated they had walked 16 miles already. The sun was lower in the sky and so far it was uncomplicated trip.

The river was always running along beside them which gave them sounds of rippling water. Along the road fishermen were casting from the shore for fish. Joseph was able to buy a cooked fish from one of them to eat later. Calm and peacefulness was with them. The donkey followed behind them with his head down but he kept the pace. The day continued on until the sun lowered in the sky about to fall behind the horizon. Joseph was aware of this road and knew of some caves in the area. He scanned the landscape for the rugged hillside that contained scattered caves throughout them. He knew that a cave would be safer. Suddenly a cave very low to the road appeared. A large tree was in front of it. Joseph tied the donkey up to the tree then he walked into the cave. It was a shallow cave just what he was looking for. He looked carefully through it to make sure no snakes or small animals were inside. He came back out of the cave and waved at Mary. She took the blanket off the donkey and brought it inside. She arranged it carefully so it covered the coolness of the ground. Joseph brought in the food and water which Mary arranged at the edge of the covering. Then he took the donkey down to the water so he could once again drink after the long afternoon walk. He walked back with the donkey and once again tied him to a tree. It was starting to get dark and Joseph went back into the cave. Mary had the fish, fruit and vegetables laid out for the small dinner they were to have. Joseph asked Mary if she was able to continue in the morning. She looked at him with loving eyes and said, "My dear we go with our Lord because he is with us. I will be fine." They curled up together on the blanket and pulled all the ends around them for warmth. Joseph could feel the enlarged stomach on Mary and he could feel the baby's movement. "Dear Lord," he whispered, "Please let us get there in time."

The next morning seemed to come very quickly as they were both so tired. The sunlight of the early morning was bursting through the cave's opening. Joseph quietly arose and gathered all the items that he needed to pack. He left the food out so they could have an early morning meal. He went out of the cave and untied the donkey and together they went to the river. The donkey lapped up the cool, refreshing water while Joseph walked out into the river. He cupped his hands and drank and then rinsed off his body. He looked back at the cave and saw Mary waving at him. He tied the donkey back up and went back to eat and help Mary pack the last few pieces of food for later. The days passed, as they walked along the river.

Joseph looked into Mary's eyes. He could see the tiredness and unrest in her eyes. He could see the weight of the baby was slowing her down. This would have to be a day that they had to make as much distance as possible. Joseph looked out of the cave and watched the water flowing down the river as he counted the miles in his mind… about 21 the first day, 18 the second and 20 yesterday. If his count was correct and the area they were at was about 59 mile from their home. He figured they had about 25 miles left ahead of them. This would be a day that they would have to walk about 20 miles. That would leave about 5 miles for the following morning.

He turned and took Mary's hand and together they carried the rest of the food and water skins to the donkey. It was still cool and it was still in the early part of the morning. Mary had slowed down but she was still ready to walk as much as she could. The day was much the same as each of the preceding days. As they came closer to Bethlehem, more travelers were encountered on the road. Joseph and Mary greeted them as they passed. Since Joseph and Mary were dressed in very plain clothing, and did not wear a lot of jewelry, they felt quite safe. Robbers and thieves looked for wealthier travelers to steal from. Several times during the day, Joseph would make Mary stop to rest and drink water and eat fig cakes and fruit to keep her strength up. She waded in the water to keep her feet from swelling. The day went very quickly and Joseph thanked God several times and asked that he watch over them so they would arrive in Bethlehem before the baby was to arrive.

As the day was coming to an end, and the hillsides were stretching out before them, Joseph knew it was time for them to find a safe place. They had turned away from the Jordan River and were walking inland to Bethlehem. They had filled up the water skins and took one last wade in the water just before the turn.

The donkey's hooves clopped along the dusty road as Mary and Joseph walked on. Mary's face showed the look of a tired woman. Joseph had a look of great concern. As nightfall overtook them, Joseph saw a ridge that stretched out in front of them. In the evening night he could see the lights of Bethlehem in the distant hills. A large Sycamore tree gave them the resting place he was looking for. Mary spread the blanket and together they unpacked the donkey. Joseph gave him some water and tied him to the tree. Together they ate a little of the food they had. The food supply was now very low. He made sure Mary ate as much as she wanted. He knew he could wait to eat and from the looks of the distance they were about 5-6 miles away.

The stars brightly lit the sky above them. And the light from the city was spotting the hillside and the valley. Joseph rubbed Mary's sore, swollen feet. They held each other as they went to sleep. Tomorrow they would be in Bethlehem. "Please Lord, let us make it," they were both thinking.

The morning came very quickly and it was now time to find a room to rest in. They didn't hesitate but got up and walked on. They walked together with a renewed faith. The business of the city was felt around them. Shepherds were in the field tending to their flocks, farmers were working in the fields. The city was rising up in front of them, and the noise of people talking and laughing. Roosters were crowing to the morning sky. Animals, men and women were all waking up to the morning light. It was a beautiful, glorious day.

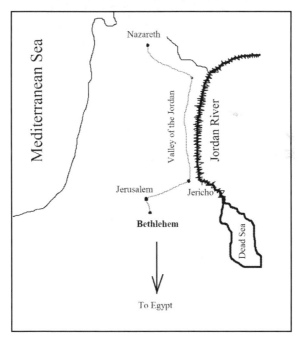

Journey to Bethlehem and map of the route they took
The map was created by Christina my granddaughter

CHAPTER 8 A

"Before I formed you in the womb I knew you, before you were born I set you apart. I appointed you as a prophet to the nations."

Jeremiah 1:5

Birth Of Baby Jesus

As they entered the outskirts of the city of Bethlehem, they saw the well. Joseph led the donkey with Mary riding on its back. Mary was very tired, her eyes were sunken and her legs and feet were very swollen. Joseph knew she couldn't go on. He helped spread the blanket under a tree and tied the donkey up. Then together they went to the well and drank the fresh cool water. Joseph filled the goatskins and took them back to the donkey. They were all exhausted. Mary sat down and took out what they had left of the food. Joseph rubbed her feet and then told her he was going to the market to get a few fresh things for her to eat. As he walked away, Mary laid down on the blanket. She could feel the weight of her stomach. She had felt a few tightening's of her stomach during the journey but now, a sudden pain stronger than the others doubled her over. She knew the time was near.

Joseph was only gone for a short time and he brought back fresh cheese, some unleavened bread, fresh fruit and vegetables. They ate together and Mary could not hide the pain she was starting to feel. Joseph saw her face and he knew he must find a place for them at an Inn soon. He jumped up and asked if she would be all right for a little while. Mary looked up and smiled. He kissed her cheek and told her he would be right back.

As he rushed away, Mary stood up to wave good-bye. She felt warmth ooze down her legs. She knew this was a sign her child was coming soon. For an instant, she felt a great worry come over her, but she looked up at the sky and sang a song of praise to her Lord.

Suddenly, a great feeling of peace and love came over her. She knew from watching other women having babies that she still had time. She tried to relax her mind and let the contractions take place. She still had a long period between pains. She kept thinking of the joy of being a mother. Soon her role would again change. A new life would be part of hers. "Oh, Lord, please give us a healthy baby." Her thoughts were consumed by this moment.

It seemed like a long time before she saw Joseph coming back. He had a very sad look on his face. As he rushed to her side, he took her hand. "Oh Mary, because of the amount of people coming into the city to pay their taxes, there is no room in any of the Inns. However, one Innkeeper offered us his stable when he learned of the baby on its way. Should we go?" "Oh Mary, will this stable be all right for the arrival of our special child? Mary looked up at Joseph and he could see the look in her eyes…time was running out. They must go to the stable. Joseph untied the donkey, put their things together and put his arm around Mary to help her up. He then put his arm around her and half carried her down the cobblestone road. The Inn was only a short distance away. The donkey followed behind them.

The Inn stable was very dark inside. Joseph found an oil lamp and lit it. He found a manger, which was used as a feeding trough. These were made from clay mixed with straw or sometimes stones held together with mud. The hollowed out in side held feed for the animals. Joseph found straw in the stable and made a bed for Mary to rest on. He spread the blanket they had on the donkey for Mary to lay on. He filled the manger with some straw and placed a piece of cloth over the straw. Mary could feel the contractions taking place on her stomach. They came closer and closer. Joseph sat down beside her and held her hand. Suddenly, Mary could feel a strong pain and she told Joseph the baby is coming. A few minutes later the baby arrived. Joseph held the baby up and gave the child a strong pat and the baby's cry filled the stable. He then looked around the stable and found a tool to cut the cord. Then took the piece of cloth from the manger and wrapped it around the baby. He knelt next to Mary and placed the baby in her arms. He whispered "It's a boy, Jesus, he's just been born." The joy overcame Mary and tears flowed from her eyes. She took the child to her breast after he seemed full she laid him in the manger. Joseph came beside her and put his arm around her. The silence in the stable was overwhelming. The animals seemed to sense what had taken place.

On a hillside near the stable shepherds were watching their flocks at night. Suddenly, and angel appeared to them and said, "Do not be afraid, for behold, I bring you good tidings of great joy. Which will be to all people? For there is born to you this day in the city of David a Savior who is Christ, the Lord. And this will be the sign to you. You will find a babe wrapped in swaddling clothes, lying in a manger." (Luke 2:10-12)

The shepherds were in awe. Could this be true? They talk among each other and several of them decided to make haste and find this baby. The night sky was filled with many stars and the moon gave them light to find the way. As they passed by the stable they heard the cry of a baby. One large star seemed to be right over the stable. As they entered the stable, they saw the manger and a baby wrapped in swaddling cloth. A man and a woman stood over the manger. The shepherds were silent, and then told them an angel told them of this blessed baby. Several sheep had followed them and lay down next to the manger. The shepherds stayed and watched in silence as the baby slept in a very peaceful slumber.

They stood and went to Mary and Joseph and asked who are you, the parents of this child that will bring the world great joy! Joseph replied that they were Mary and Joseph from Nazareth. The shepherds shook their hands and left with the sheep out into the beautiful evening night. They walked in silence back to the sheep on the hillside. They each knew that they had experienced wonderful blessed event.

Birth of baby Jesus

CHAPTER 9 A

"For God so loved the world that he gave
his one and only son
That whoever believes in him shall not
perish, but have eternal life."

John 3:16

Raising Jesus

After Jesus was born, Mary and Joseph may have found refuge in a small house in Bethlehem. Joseph, once again, took up carpentry and had a workshop behind their home. The people in and around the city would have come to Joseph to have wooden items crafted for their homes. Mary took over her duties of the household; thanking her mother in her prayers for all that she had taught her. "Hear, Israel, the Lord is our God, The Lord is one. Blessed be the name of his glorious kingdom for ever and ever." Each night she and Joseph would have prayed the same prayers as her parents had taught her. The house would have been smaller than she'd grown up in, with her mother and father. It may have been connected to a group of other homes which was like a somewhat small community. Mary always kept a pot of stew going in a small area of the house where she did the baking and cooking. She liked making bread and kept her small family well fed and clothed. They had a small garden in the back of the house for supplying their needs.

One night as dusk fell, Mary was playing with Jesus on a mat. Joseph was in his workshop finishing some wooden items. The night stars were starting to fill the sky, somewhat brighter than usual. Baby Jesus would have been around two years old and a joy for Mary to care for. Suddenly, Mary heard voices coming from the street in front of their house. She opened the door and saw three camels, each with a magi riding high, on each camel. She watched as they came down the street. Many people were following them and the crowd was whispering, "Where could they be going?" The camels turned and they were coming right to her front door. What was happening? She called for Joseph, "Come quick! We have three magi at our front door!" Joseph and Mary stood in awe as the three dressed in bright fabrics, Persian dress of trousers and Phrygian caps. They walked to the front door and saw the baby Jesus in Mary's arms. They bowed down and worshiped him. Then, they opened their treasures of gold, incense and myrrh. They worshiped only Jesus. It is possible that Mary and Joseph may have asked them how they found them. And they may have told them about the star they had followed. Since Herod would not have heard about the birth of a messiah until months later, it is possible that when he asked them to find the baby, it would have been over a year for them to find

Jesus. As the evening was darkening, the three magi left as quietly as they had come. The camels were lying down; they got on the camels and left in a different direction than they came. They did not want Herod to know where Jesus was. Mary and Joseph stood at the door and watched them go. The people in the street seemed to understand that something special took place at their home. They left in silence.

In the next few days Mary and Joseph realized that what had happened at the temple with Simeon was possibly true. When Jesus was about six week old, they brought him into the courts of the temple to carry out the requirements of the law. Simeon stepped out and saw their baby in Mary's arms and spoke loudly, "That's the One! The baby is the Messiah of Israel!" He took the baby into his arms and raised him high in the sky. Could this be true? They were the mother and father of the Messiah?

It's possible that Mary and Joseph had heard whispers out on the streets that Herod was searching for a child that was the Messiah. He had given orders to kill all boys in Bethlehem and its vicinity who were two years old and younger.

One morning Joseph woke Mary and told her an angel came to him in his sleep. The angel told him to "get up! Take the child and his mother and escape to Egypt! Stay there until I tell you, for Herod is going to search for the child to kill him." Mary, we must take Jesus and travel to Egypt. Egypt is very far away, however, we cannot let Herod kill our child!

Mary arose and started preparing for the trip. Once again they would leave everything behind and make this journey. Joseph started closing up his workshop and studying the roads that they would take. The trip would be long and hopefully they could join a caravan that would be going the same way. Joseph had calculated that it would be about 170 miles in his map measurements. Joseph told Mary to be ready at dusk, as they would leave after dark. Joseph then prepared the donkey with blankets wrapped with needed mats and food that Mary had prepared. She took a few vegetables from the garden and added figs and dates. She filled goatskin water bags with water from the community well. She collected some clothing wraps for baby Jesus. Everything was rolled and hung from the donkey and some items attached to their clothes. The day was turning into night. It was time to flee. Joseph put his arm around Mary and whispered "it's time to go."

She picked up Jesus and they went out the front door. Joseph untied the rope holding the donkey and off they went into the night.

Joseph had already told Mary that they would go a few miles out of town and reach a road that was used by caravans. They camped at night in the wayside oasis where they rested and watered the animals. They were made up of a group of people travelling together and they travelled from city to city carrying goods to be sold and traded. They carried jewelry and silks and spices most of the time. Because bandits were known to target these groups, the group leaders always invited travelers to join them. They felt the more people the less likely the bandits would attack.

The night sky was full of stars and the full moon lit the way. Mary held baby Jesus close to her chest as he slept in her arms. Joseph led the way and was leading them to a large oasis some miles from Bethlehem. He was praying that a caravan of travelers might be resting there for the night. The only sound from the cool evening night was the clopping of the donkey's hooves and the sound of their sandals on the road. After several miles Joseph stopped and heard sounds of voices, he looked back at Mary and smiled. The donkey that Joseph was leading gave out a loud hee-haw in the night silence. A donkey from a distance returned the same sound. Joseph now felt that they would be able to have a safer trip. As they came over the hill, they could see the campfires burning and the tents that protected the group of people from the night's predators. The camels were laying around the edge of the oasis in peaceful rest. Out of the darkness a man appeared saying, "Shalom!" Joseph asked where they were heading. The man said to all the cities on the way to Egypt. Joseph asked if his family could join the caravan. He nodded yes and led them to the campsite. Mary was suddenly less scared and realized that Joseph was making sure they were safe and that baby Jesus would be protected from being killed.

Each day they walked and they make friends with other travelers. They realized that many other families also were fleeing with their families to Egypt. Everyone helped each other and at each oasis the women would prepare food and the men would care for the animals and set up the tents for their families. Fires were started to prepare meals and for warmth from the cool evenings. They burned all night long. Each night they would all bathe in the cool waters at the oasis. The women also washed the dirty clothes on the edge of the rocks. It was a travelling community for the ability of getting from city to city, stopping at each oasis as they travelled along. They would be able to walk about 12-14 miles a day and as Joseph figured, they would be in Egypt in about 16-18 days, depending on the weather.

Mary and Joseph found the journey somewhat comforting as each step got them closer to Egypt and away from the scare of Herod's threat. The caravan also spread news from city to city. They both knew that the people along the way had no idea it was their baby Herod was looking for. It is not known what city they set up another household, but possibly near Cairo. However, with Joseph's carpentry skills they would have been able to once again let them live in a family setting. However, they would have a bit of culture change, as the language spoken in Egypt was different than in Bethlehem. It is thought the Egyptians spoke Afro-asiatic language, somewhat different from the Hebrew language they knew. I feel they lived a very quiet life and Mary once again went to the well for water and kept her family well fed and clothed. As they needed to keep Jesus very protected, I believe they kept to themselves and continued to raise Jesus in the Jewish faith. The years would have passed and possibly about the times Jesus was 4 or 5 years old, news was brought to the area through travelers that Herod was dead. An angel, once again, appeared in a dream to Joseph and said, "Get up! Take the child and his mother and go to the land of Israel for those who were trying to take the child's life are dead." Once again, they packed up food and clothing for the trip back to their homeland. This time they didn't have to hide with the news of Herod's death. Many other families would be making the trip to Israel and the surrounding areas. Joseph had heard that now Archelaus was reigning in Judea so they were afraid to go there. They went to the district of Galilee and back to the town of Nazareth. Mary would have been joyful to be going back to her family and friends. Joseph would have planned the trip and it would have been about 260 miles. It would have been a much easier trip as Jesus was older and would be able to walk along with them and the donkey carrying their needs. They would have once again joined a caravan and went from city to city and camped on the outskirts at the oasis. As they got closer to Nazareth, I know they would have felt a comfort knowing that the after walking 25 to 30 days they would be back with their family and friends. As they got closer to Nazareth, they were all very tired and felt the journey was about over. As the city of Nazareth was ahead of them, Mary was in a hurry to knock on the door of her parent's house. As the door opened, she saw the look on her mother's face. It was over 5 years since she last saw her. They grabbed each other and tears were in their eyes. She introduced Jesus to her mother, a grandchild she was seeing for the first time. Anne called out to Joachim and he came running. Joy was overflowing as they all hugged and talked about what had happened in the past few years. Mary took Jesus with her to the well to get them fresh water. She was so happy seeing some of the friends she left behind. She was excited about showing off her son Jesus too. Joseph and Joachim cared for the donkey and talked about reopening his house for them to begin their life again. Anne was preparing a wonderful meal to celebrate their return. Prayers of thankfulness were said and this was the beginning of a journey that lasted for the rest of their lives.

Life took on a sense of normal routine. Both Mary and Joseph were once again putting a home together. Joseph set up his carpentry business and Mary worked in the home and returned her son back to the Jewish faith. Jesus would have attended a synagogue school and learned the Hebrew Scriptures and the letters of the text. He already spoke Aramaic and now he was learning about the history of his people. Every Jewish girl and boy would have studied the Torah and become obedient to the Jewish faith. Mary and Joseph would have taught Jesus the rituals of the faith. The Sabbath was important and the annual feasts and fasting became an important part of his live. The laws of Moses gave Jesus obedience in his life. Mary and Joseph had a joy brought into their lives watching Jesus grow in his faith. Luke 2:40 tell us "and the child grew and became strong; he was filled with wisdom and the grace of God was upon him."

When Jesus was about 12 years old, Mary and Joseph took him to Jerusalem to celebrate the Passover. This was in remembrance of Israel's escape from slavery in Egypt. Fifteen hundred years had passed since God set his people free. This was in important year as Jesus was about to be 13, the year that obedience to the law, a ceremony of the bar mitzvah (son of the covenant) would take place. In preparation for this event in his life, they took him to celebrate this festival. They all traveled to Jerusalem with a group of people. It was about 6 miles. Everyone was in a happy mood and the children and adults look forward to the Passover celebration. The day was filled with food and singing and giving thanks. As the day was ending they all gather and start back to Nazareth. Suddenly, Mary discovered Jesus was not in the group. She called to Joseph "Where is Jesus?" They immediately left the group and went back to Jerusalem. They searched all that evening and finally found Jesus in the temple perfectly safe. A group of religious teachers gathered to discuss the law and Jesus sat with the students. He listened and he asked many questions, as rabbis in training had a right to do. Many in the group were astonished at the questions he was asking. Because of the religious training he was able to ask questions that revealed his spiritual understanding.

Mary and Joseph watched as they saw what their son was capable of doing. Mary went forward and spoke directly to Jesus, "Son, why have you treated us like this? Your father and I have been anxiously searching for you." Since it would have taken them one day to get to Jerusalem, and one day for the festival, and now one day to walk back to Nazareth, this caused them a longer time away from their home than they had planned. They let Jesus know they were upset.

The next few years Jesus continued to grow his religious learning and also following in Joseph's skill with carpentry. Both Joseph and Mary watched as he began to be known around the area. He started speaking to crowds as he traveled around the countryside. He was known as Jesus, son of Mary and Joseph – the carpenter. Between his travels he would also have been a great help to his father creating beautiful pieces of woodwork. Mary and Joseph were very proud of their son and the great wisdom he had learned as he grew into his adult years. He was always concerned about people and had a great unselfish love to give his family and friends. People came from all over the area to hear him speak. His name was becoming well known over the lands.

I believe that Jesus might have been close to 20 years old, when Joseph passed away. Since Joseph spent most of his time in the back yard doing his carpentry work, I feel either Jesus or Mary found him slumped over his work bench. The Bible never mentions Joseph when Jesus is traveling around the country sides, with his disciples. I know Mary's heart would have been broken and she would have needed Jesus to help her heal. The disciples would have held her in high esteem, as she was the mother of Jesus. It is documented in the Bible that she and many of her family members followed Jesus as he preached throughout the country sides. She was always in awe at the groups of followers that came to see him and hear his words. She especially liked spending time with Mary Magdalene, who was always in the crowds and around the disciples in the evenings. Mary's life had once again changed and she found traveling the county sides helped her heal.

She saw Jesus change water to wine at a family wedding. She would have seen him heal lepers. Her son had grown into a peaceful and loving man. She and Joseph were always so proud of their "special" son, given to them, as a gift from God.

The three Magi at their front door

The flight to Egypt with baby Jesus

Jesus taken out of the temple by Mary and Joseph

CHAPTER 10 A

"I consider that the suffering of this present
time are not worthy to be compared with
the glory that is to be revealed to us."

Romans 8:18

Good Friday
(2,000 Years Ago)

The sun rose and woke Mother Mary and Mary Magdalene from their sleep. They had spent the night a short distance from Jesus and his disciples. They were near Bethpage and Bethany and close to the Mount of Olives. They were following Jesus and the disciples into the city of Jerusalem for Passover. They ate some dried fruit and broken pieces of bead. They also shared drinking water from a goatskin pouch. Several of the disciples came to them and told them that Jesus was speaking on the side of the hill near where they slept. Both Mary and Mary Magdalene had spent the last few days with a group of people that were also making the trip to Jerusalem. They had enjoyed being together with Jesus and the disciples. As they climbed the stony hillside, they were anxious to hear what Jesus had to say. The hillside was filled with followers and Jesus' voice filled the air as he gave them parables for them to live by. Suddenly Mary became very concerned as Jesus ended his speech by saying, "I tell you that to everyone who had, more will be given, but as for the one who has nothing, even what he has will be taken away. But those enemies of mine, who did not want me to be king over them, bring them here and kill them in front of me." (Luke 19: 26-27)

Mary could not believe what she had heard. Jesus, her son, never spoke of killing. What was happening? As Jesus came down the hillside, he came past Mary and Mary Magdalene and looked directly into his mother's eyes. He spoke quietly. "It has started." What did he mean? Her son was acting strange. She looked at Mary Magdalene, who also seemed to be not sure of what had just happened. They followed down the hillside along with all of the followers. Jesus led the group as they approached Bethpage and Bethany. At the hill called the Mount of Olives, Jesus stopped and spoke loudly to two of his disciples, "Go to the village ahead of you and as you enter it, you will find a colt tied there which no one has ever ridden. Untie it and bring it here. If anyone asks you why you are untying him, tell him the Lord needs it." Mary looked over at Mary Magdalene and whispered, "What is my son doing? What does it mean that *it* has started? Why is he asking for a donkey?" Mary Magdalene laughed and replied, "He wants to enter the village on a donkey to start the Passover feast." Mary smiled back;

however, inside she knew this was not her son's personality. Something was different.

The disciples came back with the donkey and all of the followers gathered around and put a cloak on the donkey, and put Jesus upon the donkey. Many followers ran ahead and threw cloaks on the road and gathered palm branches. Yelling "Hosanna, Hosanna and Hosanna in the highest." Mary Magdalene grabbed Mary's hand and said, "Come! Let's go ahead and watch Jesus as he enters the city." Mary's heart beat faster as she rushed forward and heard all the voices of the people who were now building in great numbers. This was her son, who was now being praised! People were coming from everywhere on the roadside shouting: "Blessed be the king who comes in the name of the Lord! Peace in heaven and glory in the highest!"

Mary and Mary Magdalene ran along with the crowds that constantly kept building. Everyone was joyfully shouting and waving palm branches before Jesus as he rode past them. Suddenly, he disappeared in the crowd and they decided to go into Jerusalem to meet some friends and do some shopping. It was Friday and in a few hours Passover would be starting. They would find Jesus and the disciples before sundown. Mary had many friends in Jerusalem. It is possible that she spent Passover with them. However, some think Mary Magdalena may have found the disciples and Jesus and had Passover with them. It may have been Mary Magdalene who found Mary and told her of the arrest of Jesus. Together they ran to the court around the Temple. They heard the yelling from the Fortress of Antonia. Crucify! Crucify him! Crucify Jesus! She and Mary Magdalene looked through the crowd for the disciples. They were not around. Suddenly, Apostle John appeared. He was sobbing and trying to tell them what had happened to Jesus. Mary was unable to understand what he was saying. What had her son done? Why did they want him crucified? John took both of them on each arm and turned toward the rocky hill outside of the city. It took them sometime to get there, as the crowd was angry and yelling terrible things about Jesus. Since the town was filled for Passover, the streets were almost impassable. They looked over and saw a man covered in blood with a wooden cross strapped to his arms a crown of thorns was on his head and his body was covered with strap marks from the flogging that was done to him. Mary and Mary Magdalene did not recognize him; however, John assured them that it was Jesus. Mary was horrified.

John watched as Mary Magdalene took Mary into her arms. They wept together, and Mary Magdalene whispered to Mary "We don't know why this is happening, but we must trust in God." Together they said a prayer and started wiping their tears away. John took one side of Mary and Mary Magdalene took the other side. Together they supported Mother Mary as they followed the crowds.

Good Friday, Jesus entering Jerusalem on a donkey.

CHAPTER 11 A

"Jesus called out with a loud voice, 'Father, into your hands I commit my spirit.' When he had said this he breathed his last breath."

Luke 23:46

Good Friday
Beneath The Cross

(2,000 Years ago)

John led Mary and Mary Magdalene up the rugged hill to the area that was called The Skull. As they looked up, they saw three crosses with men strapped to them. They heard a voice that was familiar to them say, "Father, forgive them, for they do not know what they are doing." The voice came from the body strapped to the closest cross. Mary cried out "Jesus, my son! What have they done to you?" His eyes focused on her. She felt the great love between a mother and her son. Her heart was broken. What could she do? Why had this happened? How can I stop this? His face showed the agony of what had happened to him. Mary looked around for help. Next to her were Mary Magdalene and John. It was possible that her sister whose name was not given but was possible Salome. Also, Mary the wife of Clopa, who was the mother of Apostle James, was next to her.

They all felt the grief that Mary was feeling and it showed on their faces. Mary looked at each of them with a look that she needed help. They all stood facing Jesus as his body hung with five-inch nails hammered through his wrists. His clothes had been stripped from his body and he only wore a loincloth. His head was crowned with a circle of thorns. His legs were pushed so the knees bent slightly and his feet were nailed into place. A written notice was above him, which read: "This is the king of the Jews." This man with so much love and peace was hung to die in front of his followers and family. They could not help him as the soldiers paced around the front of the cross. Their shields held high, they seemed to be unsure what might happen.

Two other men, both criminals, were hung on each side of Jesus. One of the criminals who hung there hurled insults at him. "Aren't you the Christ? Save yourself and us!" The other criminal (rebuked) him, "Don't you fear God, since you are under the same sentence? We are punished justly, for we are getting what our deeds deserve. But, this man has done nothing wrong. Jesus, remember me when you come into the kingdom."

Mary looked up at Jesus and heard him speak back to the criminal. "I tell you the truth today. You will be with me in Paradise." The time seemed forever as Mary and his followers watched Jesus' body lose strength and the blood drained from him. Suddenly, Jesus looked at his mother and said, "Dear woman, here is your son." Then he turned his head toward John and said, "Here is your mother." John put his arm around Mary as she wept at what he said. The hours passed and the crowd covered the hillside. Crucifixions were usually never viewed by the local citizens as it was a horrific sight. However, this day was different. Word was passed around that Jesus, known as the Son of God, was hung on a cross. Everyone was interested to see what he would do. They came from Jerusalem and all the surrounding areas. It was a peaceful and quiet crowd. They were in awe of the sight they were witnessing. It was about the sixth hour when Jesus cried out with a loud voice. "Eloi, Eloi, Lama Sabachthani." (My God, My God! Why hast thou forsaken me?)

A short time later the look on Jesus' face showed that the scripture was to be fulfilled, and he said, "I thirst."

The soldiers brought forward a vessel filled with wine vinegar. This was thought to be provided by the women of Jerusalem as a final act of mercy for the condemned who were to die. They raised a sword that had a cloth ball which had been soaked in the mixture. Jesus put his mouth on it and then refused it. Mary heard the soldiers mocking him and their voices yelled, "If you are the king of the Jews, save yourself." The rulers even sneered saying "He saved others; let him save himself if he is the Christ of God – the chosen one." Jesus bowed his head and said, "It is finished."

Mary had stood below the cross for about six hours. She was in a shocked tiredness when she heard him speaking. This was the day that would change her life forever, and she could do nothing to save her son. She suddenly realized he was about to die! Darkness came over the whole land. The sun stopped shining and the curtain of the temple was torn in two. Jesus called out in a loud voice,

"Father, into your hands I commit my spirit." When he said this, he breathed his last breath.

Crucifixion of Jesus with Mother Mary, family
and friends beneath the cross.

CHAPTER 12 A

*"Now is your time of grief, but I will see you
again and you will rejoice, and no one will
take away your joy."*

John 16:22

After the Death of Jesus

John put his arm around Mary and took her down the rugged hill. She leaned on him as her body was exhausted. The women who were at her side and many of Jesus' followers were behind them. As they walked a man came out of the crowd and whispered to John. Mary knew him as Joseph, who was a member of the council. He was a good and upright man. He came from the Judean town of Arimathea and he was waiting for the kingdom of god. When he finished whispering to John, he walked away in a hurried manner. John looked at Mary and told her that Joseph was going to Pilate to ask for Jesus' body. She felt a relief come over her, as she hadn't thought about what should be done.

John took Mary and the women to his house so they could rest and have a prepared meal to restore their bodies. They were all very silent. Still not believing what they had seen. Sleep came to them very early.

The sun awakened them as it shone through the window. It was the day of Sabbath. This was a day of rest. Mary Magdalene rose and went and put her arms around Mother Mary. They held each other for several moments. John had rose and went out before the women awoke. They were alone. Her sister Salome and Mary, the wife of Clopas were still asleep in another room. Mary looked at Mary Magdalene and asked, "How could this have happened?" Mary Magdalene answered, "It was written, and time will give us the answer."

Together they busied making some food that all could eat together. Bread, fruit, and a vessel filled with wine were set out. The door opened and John and Joseph entered with news. They all gathered at the table to eat and hear what he had to say. Joseph took the body of Jesus down from the cross, wrapped it in linen cloth and placed it in a tomb cut in a rock in which no one had yet been laid. John then said," It is preparation day and the Sabbath will begin soon."

The women who had come with Jesus from Galilee followed Joseph and saw the tomb and saw his body laid in it, wrapped with a clean linen cloth and the crown was still on his head. Mother Mary knelt next to his body and reached over to hold his hand, and whispered "Good bye dear son." When they started home they looked back and saw many soldiers roll a large rock over the entrance of the tomb. Two of them stood guard over the tomb. They rushed home and prepared spices and perfumes. They worked together to complete this task. They would anoint his body with these items. They rested on the Sabbath in obedience of the commandment.

"Remember the Sabbath day by keeping it holy. Six days you shall labor and do all your work, but the seventh day is a Sabbath to the Lord your God. On it you shall not do any work, neither you, nor your sons or daughters, nor your manservant or maidservant, nor your animals, nor the alien within your gates. For in six days the Lord made the heavens and the earth, the sea, and all this is in them, but he rested on the seventh day. Therefore, the Lord blessed the Sabbath day and made it holy."

On the first day of the week, very early in the morning, the women took the spices they had prepared and went to the tomb. As they walked along together, their hearts were heavy, they knew that they would never hear Jesus speak to them, never feel the love and peace that he gave them, never follow him through the country side to listen to him speak to the followers he had gathered. Everything around them was continuing on as if nothing had happened. The mourning doves were cooing, the sun was once again rising in the East, the breeze was blowing through the trees and people they passed as they were walking didn't seem aware of their loss and their feelings.

The tomb was located on the outside of the city walls of Jerusalem, close to the Damascus gate. As they turned the corner the, rocky cut tomb was in front of them. The soldiers guarding the entrance were gone. The large, heavy rock had been rolled away they rushed forward to enter into the tomb. Mary was in complete shock. Where was her son's body? The large rock that covered was too heavy for anyone to roll away. The guards were watching over the tomb. Who took his body? Mary Magdalene and the other women left the tomb and looked for evidence that might solve their questions. Mary looked around the tomb and saw the blood that was still on the rocky bed that his body had lain on. The other women came back into the tomb. They all had looks of disbelief. Where could Jesus' body be? Suddenly, two men appeared in clothes that gleaned like lightning. The women bowed down, their faces to the ground in fright. The men said to them, "Why do you look for the living among the dead? He is not here. He has risen! Remember how he told you while he was still with you in Galilee that the son of man must be delivered into the hands of sinful men, be crucified and on the third day be raised again?"

They looked at each other, and agreed with each other that he had told them this. Was it really true? The men disappeared and the women were again alone. Mary Magdalene and the other women agreed that the disciples must be told what they had seen and heard. They all rushed away and left Mary behind to spend quiet time in the tomb to reflect on what her son's crucifixion meant to the masses of people. He was known as the Son of God. He changed people's lives. He comforted the weak. He healed the sick. He helped the poor. He changed the minds of the sinners. He was a teacher to the masses. From his mouth came the teachings of God.

Mary recalled her son's greatest sermon. She was on the hillside when he delivered the Sermon on the Mount.

> Blessed are the poor in spirit, for theirs is the kingdom of heaven.
> Blessed are those who mourn for they will be comforted.
> Blessed are those who hunger and thirst for righteousness, for they will be filled.
> Blessed are the merciful for they will be shown mercy.
> Blessed are the pure in heart for they will see God.
> Blessed are the peacemakers for they will be called sons of God.
> Blessed are those that are persecuted because of righteousness for theirs is the kingdom of heaven.
> Blessed are you when people insult you, persecute you, and falsely say all kinds of evil against you because of me. Rejoice and be glad, because great is your reward in heaven, for in the same way they persecuted the prophets who were before you.

How could her son be crucified for what he did to help people? Why would the chief priests and our rulers hand him over to be sentenced to death by crucifying him? He was not a criminal. He did not hurt anyone. He only gave love and peace to his followers. Crucifixions were for people who were sinners and criminals! Why?

Mary knelt down and lowered her head in front of the blood stained linens with tears in her eyes she whispered, "Good bye dear son. I will miss you."

Mother Mary

CHAPTER 13 A

And Mary said, 'My soul magnifies the Lord,
and my spirit rejoices in God, my savior, for
he has been mindful of the humble state of
his servant. From now on, all generations
will call me blessed, for the Mighty One has
done great things for me. Holy is his name.
His mercy extends to those who fear him
from generation to generation.'

Luke 1:46

Mary's Final Years

Mary went back to the city to find John. The streets were filled with the Passover crowds. As she walked, she heard people talking about the crucifixion of Jesus. Many were in awe, some very angry. This was an event like no other, a teacher of God crucified! She pulled the scarf she was wearing over her face; she didn't want anyone to recognize her. She turned the corner and heard the voices of the eleven disciples and Mary Magdalene. They were speaking loudly and one of them told Mary Magdalene that they did not believe her story. They thought she was talking nonsense. Mary Magdalene said again, "his body is not in the tomb." Peter got up and raced away to see for himself. He came back and verified that it was true; the body of Jesus was not in the tomb. As they all were standing in awe, John the apostle came through the door, he took Mother Mary's hand and led her out of the upper room. He knew the responsibility that he had been given and he would care for Mary the rest of his life.

As the years passed for Mary, I believe she too would always remember the night her son was born. He was born in a manger and that night became known around the world as Christmas. She did not celebrate it the way we do, but it would have been a holy night for her. Each year I know the day we know as "Good Friday" would have left her with memories of the crowds of people singing "Hosanna" and calling out her son's name. Her heart would be filled with sadness, as she thought of her son being nailed to a cross. Since I know the heartbreak of losing a son, I can relate how Mary felt. She is a special woman and because of her and her son, we continue the Christian faith. God blessed her with a son called Jesus that for thousands of years has given the world comfort and strength. She never knew that her son would "never be forgotten." His name will live on forever.

Mary would have lived a very quiet life and would have family members and friends visit her. I'm sure her Cousin Elizabeth, mother of John the Baptist, had passed away as she was much older than Mary.

Mary would have been between her late 50's or early 60's at her death, possibly August 15, 45 A.D. Mary is thought to have lived in Ephesus with Apostle John, who cared for her until her passing. Ephesus was near

Seljuk, Turkey. Her home was on a hillside and may have been somewhat destroyed in an earthquake, and later rediscovered in 1951.

Mary was not given recognition during the first three centuries of the doctrinal debate. The early churches seldom mentioned Mary and when they did; it was in connection with Jesus' physical birth and incarnation. Around the fourth century Mary had become elevated in the belief of Christians and in the teachings of the church. It is also believe that after the death of Jesus that she may have spent time with Luke, telling him about events that took place in Jesus's life and death. The book of Luke in the Bible has the most information known about Mary.

By the end of the sixth century, many stories about Mary's death began to make their way into the teachings of the church. Gregory Bishop of Tours, who lived in France, was the first father to write and teach that Mary was glorified and taken bodily into heaven at the moment of her death. This was called the "bodily assumption of Mary". This became the official teaching of the Roman Catholic Church by Pope Pius XII in 1950. Some Theologians went on to say that when Jesus entrusted his mother to John's care, he was in effect entrusting Mary to all his followers through the centuries of the church. Mary never knew how elevated she became in the Christian faith.

A view of Mary's house that can be seen by visitors

MY STORY

CHAPTER 2 B

"By wisdom a house is built and through
understanding it is established.
Through knowledge its rooms are filled with
rare and beautiful treasures."

Proverbs 24:3-4

(1944 - My early life)

As the story was told, the night of January 28, 1944 was a terribly stormy evening. The storm that was blowing snow, causing drifting, was a great concern to my mother and father. They were not sure if they would make it to the hospital. They did however, and I arrived at 4:50 on a cold, snowy Friday morning. I was the third child, following two older brothers, Dallan and Dennis. I was given the name Sandra Leah. My mother, Laverne was of German and French descent and my father, Robert, was of Czech descent.

I grew up in rural northern Wisconsin, in a small town called Black River Falls. I lived my first few years on the outskirts of town, and then my parents moved to a 125 acre farm about five miles from town. In 1947 I was about three years old. The house that we grew up in was surrounded by a haven of Elms. They gave the farm the name Elm Haven Farm. The white house has three bedrooms, one bathroom, a living room, a dining room and a small kitchen. My mother and father lived 62 years in that same home.

My parents used to tell me a story about a family by the name of Klir, who had purchased the home through the Sears and Roebuck catalog. Ready to assemble homes through mail order were sold between 1908 and 1940. Seventy thousand homes were sold in North America. They were shipped by railroad boxcars. These kits had all the materials needed to build the houses. More than 370 designs were sold over the thirty-two year history. We heard they took teams of horses and wagons to the railroad station and brought all the materials back and dug a basement. They used the instructions that were provided to assemble it. It was a well-built house and it always kept us warm and safe.

I do not remember the first few years of my life. I was told a few tidbits of information from my baby book. Like that I was small for my age. I was always full of energy and I was a happy baby. One story told to me had to do with my mother's breadbox. This was a large, lined box that was built into the kitchen. It was used to keep flour. Since my mother made all of our bread, it was always in use. My uncle Louie came to visit us quite often. He liked to put me in the box, and then push the box back and forth. I would giggle and laugh. I thought it was a lot of fun. Also, my mother told me that one Sunday when she took me to church, I would not sit still. She told me to sit still and I spoke out in a loud voice, "I don't want to." I then took off a knitted hat I was wearing, pulled off the tassel and threw it into the aisle. My mother tells me she was very embarrassed with me. Oh, yes, then the little red boots. I can just barely remember them. My mother would push them on over my shoes. They would fold over and hook on the side. I loved these boots and I also liked to march in puddles of water. I would find the deepest ones, and I liked to let the water overflow into my boots. I knew this would make my mother mad at me.

I also liked going to the bank with my mother. One story my mother told me over and over again was a day a teller asked what I wanted to be when I grew up. I remember always being in awe of the marble floors, so I replied 'I want to scrub the floors here at the bank.' This always brought my family a laugh, especially due to the fact that I worked in the banking field over thirty years. I had a dream and I went after it.

I remember very clearly going to a small one-room school. I would walk about a mile and a half each morning, with my brothers and several neighborhood children. We attended a school called Kenyon Valley School. We walked past a creek, up a large hill and down the other side to the school. We giggled and laugh and walked through season after season; late summer, fall, winter and spring. The weather was very cold at times, but we always felt warm under our coats and mittens.

Once we arrived we each had jobs to do, before classes started. We took turns putting up the flag each day. With great care we would unfold the flag, hook it in the clips on the rope, and pull the rope, which raised the flag to the top of the pole. We each had to take turns washing the slate board in the front of the schoolroom. Each eraser had to be pounded on the school's front railing. This would get all the chalk from the pads. The boys had to take turns carrying the water from the hand pushed pump, to the water bubbler. Our dinner pails were lined up in the lunch area, ready for our lunch hour. I remember we started each day by facing the flag and putting our hands over our hearts, and then we all said the Pledge of allegiance. We had one teacher, Mrs. Peterson, who taught all eight classes.

As a first grader, I remember we were the first class in the morning, usually starting with reading. Myself, and a boy named Johnny, were the only ones in first grade. We would go up to the large desk in the front of the room and read from our reading book. The other students were either taking tests or they were working on assignments. After our time was finished, the other seven grades would follow. After eighth grade finished, then it was our turn to start over with math. Then it was time for our lunch hour. We would all hurry and eat and then we played in the back of the school. We played ball, hopscotch, marbles, and hide and seek. After lunch we would start all over again with history and science. We could hear each class go over their lessons. We did our studies while each class was in session. I remember practicing my letters with a very fat pencil. I would push so hard that I would have a blister on my finger. Once a week a music teacher visited our school and we would all sing together. Many times we would put on a skit or act in or sing in a musical. We also had an art teacher that would stop at our school and we all had art projects that we worked on.

We all helped decorate the school with seasonal pictures. We decorated the windows and put pictures around the chalkboard. Many days we had science and history projects that we all were working on together. I always remember Valentine's Day, my favorite holiday. We all made Valentine holders, which we put on the side of our desks. Then we made valentines for everyone at school, and secretly put them in their holders. When the winter was the coldest, it was always fun to get a big bunch of red valentines.

During the winter months the boys had to shovel a path through the snow out to the wooden outhouses. We had one for the girls and one for the boys. I do recall some very cold days when going to the bathroom, was not very much fun, but we all survived.

Just as our days started putting up the flag, after school finished, we had to take it down. It was harder for us to take it down, as we could not let the large flag touch the ground. We had to hold it out straight and fold it back into a triangle fashion. Repeating the folding until it was perfectly shaped. We then placed it back on a shelf, ready to be put back up the next day. We were all so proud of the flag and we enjoyed seeing it waving in the wind.

I will never forget a very cold winter day. Johnny dared me to put my tongue on the flagpole, which I immediately took up the dare. My tongue stuck firmly to the pole. At first I thought I would always be stuck to the pole, however once everyone saw how bad this was, they all helped to get me off. As I remember, it was warm water pouring over the pole that loosened my tongue. It hurt for days. I never did that again!

We all worked together, played together and we always helped each other out. Life was free and easy. Each night after school, we had chores to do on the farm and our parents taught us the value of hard work.

I went through the fifth grade at this school. I had always wanted to be in the band, my parents got me a trumpet and then I didn't want to wait any longer to go to the middle school in the city. My mother went to the school board and they allowed me to go to Junior High School in the city. My life was now going to make a great change.

Dallan, Dennis and I

Dressed for church

I was small for my age

CHAPTER 3 B

"Behold, children are a heritage from the Lord, the fruit of the womb a reward."

Psalms 127: 3

August 1957-1962

The bus pulled up to the high school. My heart was pounding. I looked down at my class schedule. Every class was in a different room. How would I be able to find all these rooms? As I got off the bus, I looked over at my brother Dennis, he smiled at me. He was used to this routine. He had told me ahead of time what building to find my locker. As I looked around at all the students, a fear came over me. How would I ever exist in this large mass of students? I had fifteen minutes before the first bell would ring. I raced to the building, found my locker. I threw in my jacket, grabbed my school bag and books and raced to my first class.

This was to be the beginning of a wonderful memory. I tried out for cheerleading and made the squad. I played trumpet in the junior band. In the first few months I made many new friends. One friend that I will never forget is Linda. She lived in the city, and I lived in the country. I would stay at her house after school on nights that we would have cheerleading practice. I would than ride home with my mother; she worked at a retail store on Main Street.

School was fun for me. The late 50's and early 60's were a great time to be growing up. Our football team was one of the best in the area. Our band was always one of the best in the state. I switched to French horn and sang in the choir, played in the orchestra and found that classes of history, science, math, English, speech, typing, gym, biology, made up my life for the next six years. As I would learn years later, this was a fun time of my life.

I have many fond memories of my high school days. I loved being a cheerleader. I loved football and enjoyed Friday night games. We had pep rallies after school and then went to field where we were to watch combat of the two teams. The air was always crisp and full of team spirit. One game I will never forget I had on my black and white saddle shoes, my black cords, and a fluffy white sweater. Our colors were black, white, and orange and we were the Tigers. The first play of the game the players came down the field, and headed right towards us. All the other cheerleaders were smart, they ran backwards. I took another path. As I turned around, the player carrying the ball and a player chasing him landed right on my leg. I didn't want to get my outfit dirty, so I tried to stand up. I heard a strange sound. I was so embarrassed, this happened right in from of the stands, me with two football players on top of me. I stood up and I was covered with mud! The team doctor checked me out, and as he turned my leg, I felt the pain. He told me to go to the hospital. I told him I couldn't I had to march in the band at half time. But, I never did, as the pain was too bad. At the hospital the x-rays showed a broken bone. I had to go to the dance after the game on crutches. I was on these wooden sticks for around six weeks. It was not always fun, however I got to ride in the homecoming parade on a special float.

My best friend Linda and I had many special times. One time we were in a charitable fashion show. We were the jokers. We wore big flour bags and wore rhubarb leaf hats. The flour bags represented the hottest dress style "the sack dress". Our pictures made the newspaper. I have not seen her in many years, but I still think of her and the fun we had. During the summer months, I had a great job. I worked at a cafe on the outskirts of town. This was a very busy place, as it was a bus stop, and a taxi company was located on the side of the café, and a root beer stand that opened every summer. Several other girls and I worked in the root beer stand and the café. We cooked the food and delivered it, sometimes on roller skates. This made my summer so much fun. This looked exactly like Fonzie's restaurant in Happy Days and, as I remember, I was paid $1.25 per hour.

My mother and father were of the Methodist faith, and brought us up to know this religion. I was baptized at a very young age and went to Sunday school each week. Each week we would read stories, color, and learn about Jesus. I remember when I was about 12 years old I was chosen to be a flower girl for a special service. Around Memorial Day each year, the church was decorated with baskets of Lilacs and it was a time to rejoice the coming of spring. Four of us wore long sheer dresses and had a circle of Lilacs in our hair. We each carried a basket of Lilacs. The fragrance of these flowers filled the church. We led the choir and ministers into the church. During the service we recited Psalms from the bible. Because many of the congregation was made up of farming people, much of this service was dedicated to thanking God for a rainy planting season, a long growing period, and a fruitful harvest. One song we sang:

See around us the hand of God
Revealing new glory coming forth,
Out of the sod,
Fields of flowers,
Seeds from trees,
Streams and hillsides,
Torrents of rain,
Mighty refrain,
The hand of God.

I felt the breeze through my hair, as I hung upside down on my swing. The ground below me was a blur, as I flew up and down. My father made a swing for me using a long rope that he slipped about a two foot hollowed out pipe through. He made the length of rope even on both sides and knotted each side to a branch of a tree. The elm tree that it was hung from was a short distance from the house. I loved swinging and I thought I was a trapeze artist. I could swing high and I liked hanging by one leg. I dreamt of joining the circus and swinging at the top of the circus tent. I spent many years enjoying that swing.

One of my fondest memories of summer was lying on a blanket out in the yard as the evening dusk filled the sky. I watched as the stars appeared as the sky darkened. I always enjoyed the stars that twinkled and watched as the 'falling stars' dropped from the sky. As the evening sky was totally dark, thousands and thousands of stars filled the sky. Because we had no city lights, the heaven filled with stars was gigantic. Many times my mom would come out and lay on the blanket and we tried to find the big and the little dipper. Also, the lightning bugs (fireflies) filled the evening night. I loved chasing them and catching them in a jar. The fireflies produce a chemically cold light called bioluminescence from their lower abdomen and these beetles are about the size of a paper clip. The light is used to attract mates and both male and females light up. The colors that they transmit are yellow, green, or pale reds. They don't sting and don't fly very fast and their lifespan is about two months in the summer.

One spectacular night sky event that I witnessed was when I was around 17 years old. It was a very cold evening in February. The snow made a crunchy sound from the tires on the car. A friend was driving me home, after I was cheering at a basketball game. Suddenly bright lights were reflecting out of the rear view mirror. I looked out the back window and I said "It's the Northern Lights." They were also known as the Aurora Borealis. We stopped the car and lean up against the back of the car for about 20 minutes, watching the colorful event. The colored lights of yellow, green, pink and light blue were dancing across the dark night sky. The movements were up and down in a rhythmic movement. This happens when the collisions between electrically charged particles from the sun enter the earth's atmosphere. The lights are seen above the magnetic poles of the northern and southern hemisphere. The winter months are when they are mostly viewed, especially on cold clear nights. Most people don't get to see them in a lifetime.

The summer also brought great fun at the creek. The stream of water wound through the farmers' lands. We always played under the bridge. My brothers and many of our local friends built a dam so it would be deep enough for all of us to swim in. Our voices always filled the air as we splashed each other and cooled off from the hot summer days. I will always remember the babbling sound of the creek.

In the winter we all headed for a hill on our neighbor's farm. We pulled our sleds and took our skis to the top of the hill. Over and over we flew down the hill and then trudged back up to the top. I remember I had a pair of red skis and also a sled. We always waxed the runners on the sled and waxed the skis to make them go faster. All the neighbor kids came to the hill for fun.

Our mother and Dad made sure my brothers and I belonged to 4H Club. This is a youth organization administered by the National Institute of Food and Agriculture for the United States Department of Agriculture. The mission was to engage youth to reach their fullest potential in citizenship, leadership, responsibility, and life skills. The name represents four personal developments of focus: head, heart, hands, and health. The motto was "…To make the best better!" The slogan was "Learn by doing." This foundation began around the beginning of the 20th century. The pledge was:

'I pledge my head to clearer thinking,
My heart to greater loyalty,

My hands to larger service
And my health to better living,
For my club, my community, my country, and my world.'

My brothers and I attended monthly meetings and leaders in the community taught us topics that would help us in our everyday lives. Also, they helped us prepare for the county fair. My brother's groomed calves and cows to enter, and I learned how to sew and bake to prepare me for my entries. We all won many awards and looked forward to the end of summer to show off what we learned. I looked forward to my sewing entries as not only did I enter different categories, but also we modeled our own entries. I remember in my senior year, I made a strapless pink dress with a white and silver overlay and a pink bow. I wore it to the senior prom.

My mother also encouraged me to enter beauty contests. I was in the 'Miss Jackson County' and in area run-offs for 'Alice in Dairy-land' and 'Miss Wisconsin'. I never won, however it taught me confidence and poise. I will never forget one Saturday I was in a small town, Sparta Wisconsin; I went for an area run-off to qualify for the final event of 'Alice in Dairy-land'. I was in the first car of the parade that was about an hour long. I rode down the street in a red convertible and waved at the crowds of people lining the street for the dairy parade. The winner of this contest would represent all the dairy products from Wisconsin all over the world. It was a paying job and still exists in Wisconsin. Once I was at the end of the parade, the two guys driving the car took me back to the A&W Root Beer Stand and bought me a root beer float. Life was so simple in the 60's in Wisconsin.

Our parents taught us that it didn't matter if we won or lost, they just wanted us to experience as much as they could give us, so we would have a better life than they had. Because the experiences they gave me, at the awards day before I graduated from High School, I received the Adele Barber award for community service and music talents.

CHAPTER 4 B

"Build houses and settle down. Plant gardens and eat what they produce."

Jeremiah 29:5

Living on the Farm
(1947-1964)

'Come, Boss! Come, Boss!' my voice echoed over the hillsides of my family's farm. The farm was 125 acres and had a hill on the far side of the land. This is where the cows usually grazed. I always climbed up on the windmill that was on a small hillside behind our farmhouse. It was a job that needed to be done around 4 or 5 o'clock each day to get the cows home for evening milking. I always wonder why dad taught me to yell 'Come, Boss. I could only guess the cows were called Bossies. I liked doing this job, climbing up on the windmill and seeing all the land and feeling the breeze through my hair. I liked looking up at the large blades that converted the wind into energy by means of vanes called sails. These blades turned in a circular motion that turned slowly in low winds and the sails regulated them in high winds and when the directions of the winds changed. The tower gearbox and crankshaft converted the rotary motion into a downward stroke through a rod to the pump cylinder below. This pumped the water up to a spigot that the water came through.

As I clung to the metal crossbars, I could watch the cows as they lined up one after the other. Usually, one cow would hear my calling and they knew this was the signal for them to come back to the barn. The cows had worn a path that wandered through the far side of the land and through an area that had a lot of trees. They would walk up several hills and around a sharp curve towards home. I was always amazed that they knew what to do. Once I saw them coming, I climbed down and took the basin that held the water and put my hands under it and drank the cold, clear water. Each family member living on a farm had daily jobs to do. The cows had to be milked early in the morning and late in the afternoon.

The roosters crowing always told us it was time to get up. My brothers would help my father with the cows. They had to be put into the barn and each cow had a holding area for milking. They would be given hay and grain to eat and then a belt was put around their mid body and a milking unit that held the milk was hooked on. The milk holder had four separate units that were attached to the cows' udders. The udder is a mammary gland that produces milk. This gland collects the milk until it is time to milk and for calves to drink from. A suction pressure pulled down and the milk was pushed into the unit that is collecting the milk. Once the cow released all of the milk, the unit was taken off and the milk was put into a refrigerated vat. A large refrigerated semi-truck took the milk to a processing center and picked up this milk each day.

My father had about 12 to 15 cows to start and he grew the herd to about 20 Guernsey cows. The Guernsey cows are a breed of cattle used in dairy farming. The cows are a brown color with white markings. They are particularly known for their rich flavored milk. The average cow produces about 15,000 to 16,000 pounds of milk per year with 4.5% fat and 3.2% protein in each pound. The Guernsey cattle are known to produce the highest percentage of vitamin A in the milk of all breeds of dairy cattle. Cows spend almost eight hours a day chewing their cud. This plus normal chewing of their food can make each cow have about 40,000 jaw movements a day. Cows have four stomach compartments, for processing their food. When they take the first bite, they chew enough to moisten the food. Once they swallow this food it is mixed with other acid liquids which soften the food to small balls of food, called a cud. This cud comes back up to the cow's mouth where it is re-chewed and swallowed again. Cud chewing is often an indicator of the amount of milk a cow will produce. Cows, goats and sheep all chew their cud.

We also had chickens, and each spring we would get about 200 to 300 little yellow fluffy baby chickens. We would also have 4 to 6 baby roosters in each batch. The roosters crowning would always be our alarm clock in the mornings, as they always crowed at dawn. Chickens are gregarious birds and live together in flocks. Individual chickens in a flock will dominate the others, establishing a 'pecking order', with dominant individuals having priority over the food access and resting locations. Nests were set up and most chickens shared the nests with each other. Most hens would start laying eggs at 16-20 weeks of age with productions gradually declining after 72 weeks. Most hens preferred to use the same nest for each incubation that takes about 21 days. Then, the hens would go to the nest lay a couth of eggs, which could be up to 12 eggs. They would sit on the nest until the eggs were all laid. They would rarely leave the nest to eat or drink. They usually stayed in the nest several days after the eggs were laid. We kept the chickens in a chicken coop near the barn and we fed them corn and chicken feed. Also, we had water bubblers through the coop for the chickens to use. We threw straw and wood shavings on the floor for the chicken to rest on.

Each spring the oats and corn were planted. The fields had to be plowed and fertilized and then the seeds were planted. Farmers were always blessed if the spring and summer were warm with lots of rain. Otherwise, the crops could dry up in the fields and the payments of selling these crops would be much less. Once the oats turned a golden color, the threshing machine would come to all the farms in the area, one farm at a time. All the farmers would come and help, as the machine would remove grains and seeds from straw and chaff. The grains would be bagged and sent away for selling. The women would make food for the men working at each farm and served lunch, usually in the yards. Two saw horses would be set up with a large board placed over the top. They were used as tables. Tablecloths were put on to cover them and the food was served off this table. They would serve sandwiches made with homemade bread, salads of all kinds, casseroles and pies and bar cakes and lots of coffee and lemonade. Everyone ate outside in the yards. This was also a social event where neighbors spent time together helping each other and talking about news events that were taking place.

My father also had acreage used to grow grass and clover that could be used to feed the animals in the winter. At the end of summer, my brothers and my father would bale this hay into round units and then it was put in the barn to use as feed during the winter months. I remember one summer when my father came to the house and told me they needed me to come and drive the tractor to get the bales of hay collected and stored before it rained. When you lived on a farm, you learn to drive a tractor at a young age. I hurried out the door and my job was to drive the tractor up and down the rows of hay bales, so my brothers would throw bales from each side onto the wagon and my father would use a hook and stack them in rows on the wagon. I loved to look at clouds and this day they were especially beautiful. Suddenly, I felt the tractor tipping sideways. My father was yelling at me. I suddenly realized I had driven the tractor wheels up a bale of hay and the tractor was on its way to tipping over. My father ran to the tractor and turned the key to stop it from running. He got me off fast and they pulled the bale slowly out from under the wheels, as the tractor fell back to the ground. I could see in my father's eyes the scare that I caused him.

We also had fields of corn and in the late summer, once the corn had ripened, we had to process the stalks and store the ears. The stalks were chopped up and stored in the silo that towered up above the barn. A machine would chop up the stalks and blow them up into the silo. The cobs of corn were stored in a shed to be used for winter feed for the animals. The weather was a very important part of the storage of the crops. If it was to rainy, the farmers were unable to get the crops stored before winter. We also had an area where we had many rows of strawberries and green beans. My mother was in charge of this. When the strawberry season was in effect she would hire my brothers and I and several neighbor children to pick them. We would get a wooden handled holder that held six quart sized wooden boxes. We would pull the stand up and down the rows picking the berries. When we took them back to my mother she would put a hole in a card for each quart of berries we picked. She would then pack the boxes in a larger unit and these she would take to town and sell. She would pay each of us by the amount of quart boxes we filled. A few weeks later the green beans would be ready. We would have a sack we would pull through the rows and again get paid for the amount we picked.

We had a large garden filled with potatoes, carrots, tomatoes, lettuce, cucumbers, onions, dill, rhubarb, sweet corn, green peppers, and many other vegetables. We lived on these during the summer and when the late summer winds became colder we had to harvest these vegetables to be used during the winter. I would help pick the tomatoes and cucumbers and mom would start canning these. The cucumbers would be canned into dill pickles and the tomatoes would be used for tomato-based casseroles and goulash. The carrots and potatoes were dug up cleaned and stored in the basement under the stair steps where it was dark and cool. Then it was time to go to the apple orchard and collect all the apples. Mom would make applesauce and can as much as she could. The rest of the apples we would clean and place each in newspaper and also place beneath the stairs. We would eat these stored produce during the winter. Mom would make apple pies, used the carrots and potatoes in stews, and the potatoes were also used by mashing and cut up and frying them. The winters were very cold but mom somehow kept us all well fed.

My mom would make four loaves of bread in a week. The house was filled with the smell of fresh baked bread. The kitchen shelves were always filled with flour; sugar, spices and we always had plenty of butter, eggs and milk. My mother could make so many things with these items. She would make pancakes, French toast, rhubarb cakes and pies, poppy seed cakes, cookies, short cake biscuits, and her specialty – cinnamon rolls, apple pies, and fruit cakes. Once every few months dad and mom would make doughnuts together. Mom would roll out the dough and use a doughnut cutter to make the holes. She would put them on a sheet and give them to my dad. He fried them in the oil and turned them once when they turned a beautiful brown. He then took them from the oil and put them on a towel for oil to be absorbed. Mom would then take the doughnuts and the holes and dipped them in cinnamon and sugar, then drizzle some with frosting she made. We would eat most of them while they were warm. When she cooked the bacon, she would pour the grease into a coffee can that she kept on the oven. She used this every time she fried or cooked food that needed oil. She was very resourceful and never threw anything out that she could use again.

We had a clothesline in the backyard and mom washed clothes once a week and hung out the clothes to dry. She hung them out even in the winter and always told me they always smelled better when they froze, and then dried. And she was right. The sound of the sheets and clothes flying in the breeze was a sound that was peaceful along with the sound of Wren singing in in the background. My brothers make bird houses in the winter and I would hold the wood when they were sawing. The saw slipped once and I still have a scar on my finger where it cut into the skin. The bird houses were made for certain birds to use. The size of the hole in the front was what determined which birds would make it a home. The Wrens house had a small hole about the size of a quarter. I named the wren that seemed to come back every year Jenny.

The phone that we had to communicate with was on the wall and we were on a party line. It had a crank on the side and a speaker in the front. Our number was 44F11, which meant the Route was 44 and the ring to call us was a long ring and a short ring. The first number after the F was for the number of long rings and the second number was the number of short rings. Since we were on a party line, other people on that line would listen to everyone else's conversations. I always had fun when my friends called. After they hung up, I stayed on the line to hear how many other people also hung up. We would call them Rubbernecks. I also used codes with my friends so the people listening would not know what we were talking about.

When I was about 13 years old, in the late 50's, we got our first black and white television. My mom's brother Ernie sold them and we were one of the first ones in our area to have one. Programs would be on only a few hours a day. I remember Howdy Doody, Lone Ranger, and the Ed Sullivan shows.

My father loved to watch the Packers and on Sundays we all watched the games with him. My brothers left the farm in the late 50's. Dallan went to Minnesota to college. And, at age 17 my brother Dennis enlisted in the Navy. I was now the only one at home with my mother and father

It was very difficult for my parents once my brothers left. I could see in my dad's face that he would now have to make some changes as the many farm chores would be too much for him. Slowly, he started selling off the herd of cattle. My parents' life was about to change. My father would stop farming and went to the city to get a job.

Views of the windmill, the flower garden, the vegetable garden along with the farm buildings and the house we lived in.

CHAPTER 5 B

"Therefore a man shall leave his father and his mother and be united to his wife, and they will become one flesh."

Genesis 2:24

(August 1, 1964)

August 1, 1964 my life was to take a change that would begin a new lifestyle for me. The wedding invitations said 7:30, however something was going wrong. What? The photographer had finished taking the pre-wedding pictures and we were all ready to begin. My mother adjusted my veil and I looked over at the bridesmaids. They were wearing long yellow dresses and each carried a long stem yellow rose with a yellow ribbon. They look just as I had imagined in my dreams. What was wrong, it was now 7:45, I was very concerned that my husband" to be" decided not to get married! What would I do? I looked in the mirror to take one last look. My dress was a long white silk dress with seed pearls on the bodice. A long train flowed down the back. My veil was separated with part of it hanging down the back and the other part pulled forward over my face. I had on long elbow-length gloves and carried a dozen long stemmed yellow roses. This was my long awaited dream day. I was nineteen years old, ready to start my new life. I heard my mother coming down the stairs; she looked over at me and said, "It's time to start the wedding." I couldn't help but want to know what the delay was. My mother explained that because of the heat, people waited outside until the last possible moment and it took the usher longer to get the guests seated. The church had no air conditioning and only fans setting around in different areas to blow air as it was close to 100 degrees. My father took my arm as we went up the stairway to the chapel. I looked up and saw the church bursting with wedding decorations. It was a candle lit service. I had candles lit on every other pew and streams of yellow and white silk ribbon trailing from each pew down to the front of the church, and yellow roses on the altar. People were everywhere. Extra chairs had to be set up in the hallway. Over 250 people were in place. I watched as the bridesmaids, one by one went down the aisle to be met and escorted to the altar by a groomsman. My maid of honor looked over at me and smiled, then started down the aisle. I could feel that my father was nervous. We started down the aisle to organ music playing. The church was very warm and I could feel my cheeks getting red as I walked down the aisle, on the white runner leading the way through the candle lit pews. I looked up and saw the altar, where my husband to be, the groomsmen, and my bridesmaids were lined up neatly, a picture of a dream wedding.

The service was traditional, with the organ music and the minister presenting the wedding vows. We had memorized our vows and I can still remember hearing my voice. I didn't sound like myself. We kissed and returned down the aisle as husband and wife. Pictures were taken.

After an evening spent with friends and family, cutting and eating cake, and walking through the tables filled with many gifts, we left on our honeymoon to Wisconsin Dells, Wisconsin. The next day we left for Chicago, where we went to a photography convention. My husband, Bruce, was a photographer and he had photos entered in the competition. Photographers and people were attending from all over the world. A visiting master photographer represented each state. We spent the next few days going to seminars and spending time with many friends and other photographers. The last night was a night to remember. That was the night that they awarded photographs ribbons for their award winning pictures. My husband won several awards and got an award for a picture I had posed for. I was dressed in an old fashion outfit and sat at a table with an oil lamp and I was working a spinning wheel. The day ended with a banquet with the guest speaker, an astronaut who was very active in the space program. After he spoke, we went up to our room to call home to our parents. When we return, as we open the door, the whole room rose and the evening speaker introduced us and asked us to come up and dance, because it was our honeymoon. Hundreds of people applauded as we danced alone. Some of our friends from Wisconsin Group had arranged this moment. It was a very exciting week for us. My husband was recognized for his talents and we had fun being wined and dined, spending time, and adjusting to our new life with one another.

On Sunday, our week came to an end and we had to return to Madison Wisconsin where we started this new life. We had both left our parents homes to begin life with one another together.

I married my High School sweetheart and we had known each other for many years before we married.

My wedding day with my mother and father

CHAPTER 6 B

*"All your children shall be to taught by
the Lord, and great will be your children's
peace."*

Isaiah 54:13

(1968 - 1989)

As I opened my eyes, I could see the blue sky overhead, clouds passing by. The breeze was blowing my hair and I felt a great feeling of being totally free. This would be the last ride we would have in this beautiful car. We had purchased this 1955 Ford T-Bird for an investment. The convertible top was hard and we would take it off and put it in our living room. The color was soft green and it had the distinct porthole on each side of the top. Now our life was about to change again. I put my hand on my stomach and I could feel the growth of a new life developing inside. What a joy I was so excited about the thought of having a baby. I had spent much time wondering what I was going to have, girl or boy. My prayers were, please God just allow it to be healthy. However if I had a choice, I wanted a little girl. As we drove along, I looked back at our life. The last four years had given my husband and me a chance to find our way in this big, busy city of Madison. He had become a very good commercial photographer by working for several studios as an apprentice, and he learned as much as he needed from this, to open his own studio. This was his dream and it now came true. I had worked in a very large department store as an assistant buyer. I worked in the jewelry and accessory department. My buyer and supervisor, Vi, was a beautiful woman and she continued to teach me how to feel good about being a woman. We had many fun and memorable moments. We all had to wear black dresses which were the dress code. We had fun going into the dress department to try on new black dresses to wear each day. Because we had the jewelry department to run I remember when pierced ears became fashionable. The salesman who first brought them to the store talked my buyer into introducing them, by having all the sales assistants pierce their ears to wear them. At that time, the only way to put a hole in an ear was by using a needle. We all shrieked and said, "That would not be fun", and however, after much pleading by the salesman...we did it by the following week. We made the bathroom on the 3rd floor our room for the exciting event. One girl had performed ear piercing on her friend and was eager to do this to us too. We each took turns and helped by holding an ice cube behind our earlobes as she pierced each ear. So simple...we wore gold studs for a couple of weeks and sold lots of pierced earrings. That was the beginning of the still popular fad.

The other great fad was heavy knee socks. The college girls would come into our department and buy 10-12 pairs to match all of their outfits for school. Everyone wore garter belts to hold up their nylons. This was a time when pantyhose became a new revolution of firsts, when they were introduced in our department, we laughed and could not believe that a woman would pull these on and wear them. But to our shock, they became the new rage. We all began wearing them. I will always remember what my mother taught me about wearing my nylons; I must never let anyone see me with a run in them. It was not proper for women to allow this to happen. Many times over the years if I had run, on my lunch hour I would buy a new pair, as I always remembered what my mother taught me.

These were the years where life was changing. Elvis Presley had begun to give everyone a new type of music. The Beatles came to America to shock us with long hair and strange looking clothes. We yelled and screamed each time we heard them sing. The war in Vietnam was on T.V. every night. Rice paddies and helicopters took over our minds and it seemed like it was many miles away. Black people, African Americans were suddenly showing us the terrible way they had been treated. Women also were coming forward to show they needed to be recognized in the working world and felt that their needs were changing.

President Kennedy was shot. Martin Luther King, Jr. was shot. Bobby Kennedy was shot. People were worried about the changing times and changing lifestyle. Our country was racing to be the first in putting a man on the moon. This was accomplished as we watched the event on T.V. Our country was young and we seemed to be showing the world about our stylish way of living. Times were a changing. And our lives were changing too.

As we drove out of the city and into the rural area, I looked out at the countryside and suddenly saw the brand new house we were about to move in to. It was ahead of us at the intersection of the road in a suburb of Madison. A beautiful white two-story house with four bedrooms, and because it had been a show home, it came fully furnished. We seemed to be so blessed, a new business; a new home; a new baby on the way.

As I went about the doing the household tasks that I needed to get done, I felt a special glow. Something was happening inside my body. I was a woman about to begin a new journey in my life. Because I was always feeling good during my pregnancy, my life had not changed a lot. I was able to live my life on a regular daily routine, which allowed me to enjoy the last nine months and spend time in the yard and the garden, I had started. I was looking forward to going out with friends and my husband's business clients for our monthly Friday night fish fry group. We met once a month for cocktails and an inexpensive dinner out, eating as much fish as we wanted. It was a very hot day.

At about 4:00, I felt a strange feeling. I went into the bathroom and I discovered I was wet and then I realized that this is what they told me about my water breaking, a term I had only heard about and now I knew what it meant. I called my husband and told him I would call my doctor and tell him what had happened. His voice was filled with an unknowing sound, "Are you sure?" "Well", I answered, "as sure as I can be." It was time to begin the last cycle to receiving our child. I called the doctor and he told me to take my time and proceed to St. Mary's hospital. Since this is your first baby, it will take a while. It was now about 6:00pm when my husband came and took me to the hospital. A nurse took us to a room and we played scrabble and I practiced Lamaze breathing. I felt extremely well. My stomach hardened occasionally and then released. The nurse came in and said I need to get you in the delivery room immediately. She said I had dilated to seven and she could see the head. I was calm and couldn't believe how fast this had gone. The cramps were now faster and faster. I told my husband I would see him soon and they wheeled me away. As I arrived in the delivery room, I could see the excitement of the nurses. A resident doctor was brought in, as my doctor hadn't arrived yet. Suddenly, I felt a very strong cramp and the doctor said push, so I pushed. The doctor then said pant and relax before the next push. Once again, I pushed and he said the head is clear. One more push and with that I could feel the body of the baby push out. I heard the doctor and the nurse talking. The doctor's voice pierced the room, "It's a girl!" I was overjoyed. Lisa Leah had entered the world on Friday, July 26th, 1968 at 10:20pm. I wanted a little girl and now I was a mother. They wrapped her up and put her in my arms. This is one feeling I will never forget. I looked down at her and knew I had a great responsibility that with this gift given to me - a child, a life, a joy of a lifetime. They told me that they had to take her away and have her checked. I would get to see her again very soon. Another nurse came to my bedside and explained that they had a situation, a barometric pressure had pushed through before a storm, causing babies to be born and the hospital had more babies delivered than they had expected. They had no room available for me. A drop in barometric pressure has been known to add a weight to the air and gases that press down on our bodies. The pressure causes women to go into labor, as it causes the membrane to rupture and labor begins. They asked me if it would be all right if I slept in the hallway. They would put screens around me. They told me that in the morning, some of the mothers would be leaving with their babies. I was so happy I said it would be fine. The nurse also told me a group of friends kept calling to the hospital to see if the baby was born, would it be alright to tell them before my husband knew? Since husbands weren't allowed in the delivery room, he still didn't know about our daughter. I told her to tell them.

The next morning I woke up to the sounds of nurses walking up and down the hallway. Breakfast was brought on a tray. They also put a small white cup with 2 pills in it, which I took. Lisa was brought up and what a blessing to hold my daughter. I had her for a few hours and then they took her back to the nursery. Finally a room was available and I was able to be alone. The evening was filled with many friends coming in to visit me. Soon the announcement was made that all visitors were to leave. I curled up and felt a wonderful comforting feeling. In the darkness, I awoke and felt myself clinging to the phone. I had it off the hook and a nurse came rushing into the room. She took the phone from my hand and asked if I was okay. I replied that I am calling God to tell him I had a baby girl. She looked at me and took my temperature and checked my blood pressure. She talked with me for a few minutes and then asked me if I could go back to sleep. I told her I could. The next morning my doctor came and spoke to me about what had happened. He told the nurse to stop giving me pills. I was too excited about being a mother to question what had happened to me.

What a joy to bring home my daughter and care for her. The days were filled with the challenges of being a new mother. The days went flying by and Lisa was smiling and growing up fast. One night, when we had friends for dinner we heard noises in the family room. Lisa was sleeping in her playpen. As I entered the room, she had crawled out of the crib and was walking to me with a big smile on her face. Lisa was about nine months old. About that same time I felt changes once again in my body. I spoke to my doctor and he checked me over. I couldn't believe what he told me. I was pregnant again! How could that be? I told my husband that I didn't want to tell anyone else right away. One Friday night we were out with the same group, from the fish fry group. One of the men said "you have a glow on your face like a woman who might be pregnant.' I said how did you know? My secret was out! Once again I was feeling great during the nine months. One night I was watching "When a Man Loves a Woman" on TV and Lisa was asleep in the playpen. My husband's brother Bob was visiting and they were in the kitchen talking. I felt a pain and then tightness. I waited and then it came stronger. I knew it was time. I went in the kitchen and told them that it was time to go to the hospital. His brother said he would stay with Lisa. It was about 9:30 and I called to tell my doctor I was leaving for the hospital. It was a cool evening. The leaves had fallen and the night sky was especially beautiful, each star was shining brightly. We arrived at St Mary's hospital and I could feel the pains were coming much closer together. A nurse took me right to a room. She checked me and said it would not be long. Once again, my doctor didn't make it to the hospital. I was in the delivery room and at 11:10 on November 5, 1969 Eric Alan was born. I was so happy. A boy! The sex of the baby could not be given prior to birth. I was full of joy. Now I had a girl and a boy.

Eric was also an easy child. At about 6 months, he started to have eczema on his skin. The doctors tested him and he seemed to be allergic to everything. When he was about a year and a half, he was sick and I took him to the doctor's office and several doctors told me to hurry and go to the hospital. They checked him over, however they didn't tell me what he had. I was scared and ran as fast as I could with Eric in my arms. They took him out of my arms and ran with him down the hall. They put needles in his arm and I stood in a complete shocked state. What was wrong? Several doctors came and one put his arm around me and said it's a big word and we have to work fast. Your son has spinal meningitis. What did that mean? They would talk to me later. We were fortunate we got him to the hospital in time and after about three weeks; he was released with no brain damage. While he was in the hospital they covered him with a substance that looked like black tar. It was for the eczema. When he came home his skin was cleared and he was once again a happy boy filled with energy.

This was a wonderful time to raise children. We lived in a community of neighbors that all knew each other. Our husbands went to work each day and we mothers took care of children and our homes. We had a park in the area and the children played there each day. We had a women's card club and we would meet once a month and play five hundred. We also had a bowling team. We enjoyed the four seasons and our children growing up together, going to school together, and spending the summers playing soccer and baseball. The 60's and 70's were the times of innocence and life was so easy. We all took turns watching each other's children and we had gardens and loved to cook in our kitchens. As a community, we all helped each other's families in everyday life events.

One day I will never forget, was in the summer when Eric was about 4 years old. I came in from gardening and asked Lisa "where is Eric?" She didn't know so I told her to go and check with the neighbors to see if he was at another house. She came back and told me no one had seen him. Some of the neighbors came quickly to our house, concerned about Eric. I went through the house and basement, and took one last look in his bedroom. He was not to be found. A large group of neighbors formed lines and we walk through the yards calling his name. The neighborhood had several empty basements, as homes were still being built. We were all worried that he may have fallen in one. After several hours I was horrified that we could not find him. We decided to go back to the house hoping he found his way home. I went upstairs to look in his bedroom, and for some reason I opened up the doors to his closet, and there he was fast to sleep. We all cheered as we were happy to know he was safe.

Lisa and Eric grew up enjoying each other's company. Lisa was outgoing and Eric was shy. The community had many families that were raising children the same age as mine. The park was in view of my kitchen window and the whole neighborhood of children had fun there all year around. Life was so much different. They all played together and we mothers never worried about someone taking them. The girls like to play with their Barbie dolls in the shelter house and the boys played baseball and soccer on the ball field. I had a bell I would ring when it was time for them to come home.

Eric loved playing baseball and soccer and was on a neighborhood team. They played scheduled games with teams from other communities. His feet were fast and he especially liked soccer. He could take the ball down the field with great speed.

My children grew up like all the other children, always outside both summer and winter. They enjoyed all of the winter activities, skating, skiing and having fun in the snow, snowball fights and making snowmen.

As Eric got older, he enjoyed playing hockey, as did all of his friends. Hockey skates, pucks and hockey sticks were always in the hall by the front door.

Both Lisa and Eric graduated from West High School in Madison Wisconsin. Lisa went on to Madison Community college and Eric went to Stevens Point College, in Stevens Point Wisconsin. He was very talented in art and was pursuing a business and graphic art degree.

I was now beginning my next life journey, as an empty nest mother. Not only had my children left, my husband and I had grown apart. He was totally dedicated to his commercial photography studio, staying at the studio day and night. It was also a time when women were caught up the Women's Liberation Movement. Women wanted to leave the homemaking behind and find careers outside of the family structure. I also found myself caught up in this movement and begin my career in banking, which I spent over 30 years working in, until retirement. All that we worked for now ended in divorce.

Top pictures is the last picture taken of Lisa and Eric
Pictures of Lisa and Eric having fun and growing up together

CHAPTER 7 B

"God is our refuge and strength, an ever present help in trouble."

Psalms 46: 1-3

September 1991

This is how Eric's story started. He was starting his senior year at Stevens Point College. He called me and told me he needed to have a yearly checkup. He asked me if he should show the doctor the lump he had on this lower leg that he got from being hit by a hockey stick during playing his favorite sports game. He told me it was hard and about the size of a quarter. He said it didn't hurt. I told him it would be a good idea to get it checked.

Then, suddenly, my life was to change; I got a horrific call from my daughter Lisa. "Mom, Eric has cancer in his leg." The doctors were going to amputate his left leg at the knee. How could this have happened? The operation was to be at 4:00pm on Friday. I was hysterical. My dear son! It can't be true. I told my daughter I would be flying home and I would let her know when I would arrive. The next couple of days were a blur. I let the people at the bank, where I worked, know what was happening. Together they helped me get a flight and gave me support as I gathered what I needed. I got a ride to the airplane by a good friend Iris. She could see the emotion and we didn't talk a lot on the way. It was Friday morning, the day I was dreading.

When I was finished going through security, I went to the departing board and the word 'delayed' was posted by my flight number. It can't be! I went to the gate and asked what was making my flight delayed. The lady at the counter wasn't sure. It was a connecting flight and it would be at least an hour and a half late. My heart sank. I was flying from West Palm Beach to Detroit, with a short layover to put more people on the flight, as its final destination was to be Madison, WI. My mind was working frantically at figuring out what time I would arrive. With the one-hour time change it would make my arrival in Madison at close to 4:00pm. I knew it would be another twenty to thirty minutes to get to the hospital. I called my daughter from a payphone and gave her the news. I told her to call the airport for my delayed arrival. We were both crying. I told her I couldn't believe that I probably won't be able to see Eric before he goes in for surgery. I told her I would see her soon. The time waiting for the plane seemed like forever. Suddenly, an argument started at the check-in counter. Four young men were yelling at the woman at the counter. It seems that they were flying to an Ann Arbor, Michigan football game that Saturday, but they had a golf game set for 4:00pm that day. They demanded to know why the plane was delayed and let her know that they would miss the t-off. They were very rude and she told them they should call on the payphone to tell their friends they would be delayed. She couldn't tell them how long. As they stomped away, I felt a strange feeling come over me and wanted to ask them, 'how they would you like to be late for their son's amputation surgery'? That experience left me with an understanding of what other people deem important.

They started boarding and I was up and away. I looked down at my watch and we were now in the air about 2 ½ hours. The hum of the airplane brought me back to my surroundings and the emotional hours that brought me onto this airplane. As I looked around at all of the people, they all seemed happy to be flying away. How could everyone be so happy and content with the hour and a half delay that occurred? I looked out the window as tears spilled out of my eyes. I didn't want anyone to see me so I kept looking out at the fluffy clouds and the deep blue sky. I couldn't stop thinking about what was going to happen this day. My son Eric's leg was to be amputated. How could this be? I heard the pilot announce that we would be landing soon and he was sorry for the delay. The plane floated out of the sky and onto the runway with a sudden touchdown followed by the taxi to the gate. The stewardess announced the plane would be continuing on to Madison. As soon as they cleaned the interior of the plane, they would begin boarding passengers that were going on to Madison. Because they were late in arriving, they asked that all passengers that were going on to Madison to remain on the plane. I looked around as everyone left the plane. I was the only one left on the plane. I suddenly felt an emotional letdown and I started to cry again. I was somewhat frozen in my seat. One of the cleaning crew, who was a woman, came to me and told me I have to leave while the cleaning took place. I looked up at her and started to cry again. I told her, "I can't leave, and I have to get to Madison." I felt her hand take mine and I looked up to see her face. She was African American with dark hair and a very peaceful looking face. She said, "Come with me" and my body suddenly, without hesitation, went with her. We walked off the plane and through a long line of people waiting to board. They were a blur of colors as we walked by them. I could see people looking at us. She had her arm around me. She was so dark next to my pasty white complexion. I was crying and I felt that she could take me anywhere. I was totally under her command. We walked down steps and through a door that indicated for 'employees only'. She sat me down at the table and put coins in the vending machines. She placed a drink and several candy bars in front of me. She then sat down across from me and said, 'Sweetie, tell me what's wrong." I blurted out that my son has cancer and they will be amputating his leg at 4:00pm and I'm not going to get there in time to see him. She took my hand and told me to cry. However, she said "Once I take you back to the plane, you have to be strong." She told me a story about her grandchild that had brain cancer, so she knew what I was going through. She told me again that I had to be strong as my family needed me and she wanted me to promise her that I would get myself together before I faced my son and my family. She once again said your son would need you to be strong. She then put her arm around me and took me past the line of people and onto the plane to my seat. She hugged me and then left the plane. The people were now boarding and I found a napkin and wrote on it…'I want to thank you for helping me". I asked the stewardess to give this to the lady on the cleaning crew and I didn't know her name. In fact, I never knew if she received the message. However, I have often thought about her and how she helped me, like an angel.

The flight to Madison was one hour long. Because the time change, I left Detroit the same time I arrived in Madison. I walked through the airport and came down the elevator. I saw my daughter and she came running to me and told me that the operation had been cancelled. I looked to the heavens and said 'thank you, Lord.'

We drove back to her apartment and on the way she told me I had to be at Eric's doctor's office at 4:00pm on Monday. Both his father and I were to be there with him. I couldn't wait to see Eric. I put my arms around him and gave him a big hug. At that time he and I were not aware of what the following Monday would bring.

CHAPTER 8 B

*"Come to me all you who are weary and
burdened, and I will give you rest."*

Mathew 11:28

Monday September, 1991

This was the day that would change our lives forever! I looked up at the clock and it was ticking away the seconds and the minutes, bringing the time closer to 4:00pm. I spoke to my ex-husband and he told me Eric's cancer had spread. He didn't want me to tell Eric because the doctor wanted to explain it to him. The most difficult part of the day was watching Eric as he was very happy and content, having no problems at all, and happy to be with me. The weekend had seemed rather normal as I saw many old friends and spent time with my family.

Suddenly, it was time to leave for the trip to the doctor's office. An air of strangeness seemed to take place in the car, as Eric seemed somewhat concerned why we were all going. I looked over at him and couldn't believe that he was sick. He looked healthy and I kept denying he could have cancer. It could not be possible.

We entered the office of Dr. Batson and the three of us said a quiet hello. He explained how difficult this was for him. He had children himself and could not image getting this diagnosis. He started by giving us the tissue biopsy taken from the lump on Eric's leg. The lump tissue had no cancer cells; however the tissues around the lump indicated cancer, a type called small cell sarcoma. The MRIs indicated many spots on both lungs. He then said Eric had around two years to live. Silence filled the room. Then, a sigh came from my son's mouth. My mind kept thinking, "No, it can't be!" I won't let it be. Please Lord this must be wrong.

Then Dr. Batson explained the choices Eric would have as he was over 21, he would make the decisions.

No chemotherapy

Chemotherapy with follow-up MRIs

The Medical Research Department of the University of Wisconsin

He explained each of these choices and told Eric he could let him know when he made his decision and if we needed to get counseling about the medical situation it was available to each of us.

He asked us if we had any questions. We were all in shock as we all nodded no in unison. Eric then stood up and shook Dr. Batson's hand and said thank you. We all left his office. As we walked, I held back tears.

The ride back to Lisa's apartment was in silence. I didn't know what to say. We all could not believe what we heard. When we got back to Lisa's apartment, when Eric was away, I explained to Lisa what we found out.

The next few days were filled with the question of what should Eric do? I spent a few hours with a cancer consultant woman who spoke with me about the situation I had with living in Florida…so far away. She asked me many questions regarding how I felt about Eric's condition. Would I get emotional when he was sick from chemo, would I be able to handle his loss of hair, would I be able to keep from feeling sorry for him, and would he see this in my face, where would I live if I moved back? All these questions seemed to confuse me. I didn't have the answers. Then, she changed the questions and told me what she had learned from many mothers. She told me many have great difficulty in seeing their sons suffer and go through the changes in their bodies. Many of them became sick also and took on a lot of the same signatory, such as loosing hair and having the same pains and nausea chemo creates. She told me that many sons told her they didn't like seeing their mothers got through this suffering. Many times it was easier for them if their mothers lived in another area so they didn't watch them suffer and try to take their pain away and keep them from living the life of a 20 year old. Young men especially in these circumstances wanted to live a life with friends and having the ability to rise above the cancer and enjoy what time they had. She asked me if I had a job and a life in Florida. I told her I did. She convinced me that by going back I could see how Eric felt about his life ahead and I if he could handle facing his challenges. I could always move back after I saw what the next few months brought.

The next few days were difficult. It was hard for me to talk with him about what choice he would make. He called Dr. Batson and told him he wanted to find out about the Cancer Research Department at the University of Wisconsin. Dr. Batson made an appointment for us and we went to learn what the treatments would be about.

We were seated in an office and then the door opened up and several men wearing white lab coats walked in. They were very confident and told Eric about the treatments. They had already seen Eric's scans and they explained to him that they had many experimental treatments. One might hold the cure for his cancer. The research department had around seven oncologists that would be involved in a part of the treatments and they felt they would all be a great help in his treatment. They explained that the drugs used were experimental and would be of no cost and the medical records would be provided to the National Cancer Institute. They gave him paper work and their business cards. They told us if he was going to join the program, he needed to sign the forms and call them for an appointment.

The next few days, Lisa and I fixed up her apartment so that she and Eric would be comfortable while they lived together. Because of the close relationship I felt sure this would work out for both of them. Lisa was to become Eric's caretaker during the next 2 1/2 years.

As I flew back to Florida, I looked out to see the blue sky and the fluffy white clouds. My heart was broken and what the counselor told me was of great concern. How would I be able to be so far away from him at this difficult time? I looked again at the clouds and said "please Lord, make this go away." The pilot announced that we would be landing soon. This brought me back to the situation I had to face; my second husband wanted a divorce.

CHAPTER 9 B

*"Ask and it will be given to you, seek and
you will find, knock and the door will be
opened to you. For everyone who asks
receives, he who seeks finds, and to him
who knocks, the door will be opened."*

Mathew 7: 7-8

(1991 – 1994)

I could feel my body shaking as I sat at my desk. I was working at a small branch bank in Delray Beach, FL. I looked up and told Deanna, a co-worker, that I have to go to the bathroom. I rushed away and down the hall and I was hoping she did not see my face. I looked at my face in the mirror. "Oh Lord, what am I going to do?" I felt so alone. I locked the door and sat down against the wall and cried. I was only back a couple of weeks from learning of Eric's fate, and now this!

I was sitting at the pool on Saturday morning when my husband walked up to me and said he had a file folder that he wanted me to open and read the information within it. He was leaving and would be back in a few days. The gate at the pool closed and he was gone. I opened it up and found documents indicating he wanted a divorce. I was, once again, in a state of shock. How could this be happening too?

I had only been in Florida for six months. I had remarried several years after my divorce and had relocated with my husband to Lighthouse Pointe, Florida. He was in the bakery industry, and his territory for selling bakery and deli equipment was changed to the state of Florida. After selling our house and having a two day auction to sell all our household items, we were off to a new life. The trip was a long one, as it was about 1,800 miles. We left with a U-Haul and my daughter Lisa and I were driving behind in my Dodge Daytona. Lisa and I had fun as we drove across the states. We especially enjoyed driving through the Smokey Mountains. I was anticipating the visits that Lisa and Eric would make coming to see me in Florida. I was so excited about this new journey of my life. The cold winter was left behind and I was now looking forward to the sunshine.

I was in the bathroom for hours, Deanna told me. She came to the door every few minutes to ask me to come out. I told her each time that I was never coming out. I remember asking God for his help. I prayed if you show me the way, I would follow where you lead me. I know that this is the day I surrendered all to God. I sat in silence and got myself back together. Deanna came again and said, "You can't stay in there any longer!" I opened the door and came out with my eyes red and my face full of sadness. She took me back to my desk and I told her and another co-worker Iris that my husband wanted a divorce and my son had been diagnosed with terminal cancer. They both hugged me and this was the beginning of a journey with each of them that has continued for over twenty years. We spent time after work together and enjoy work even more as our friendships grow.

During the next few months I had to find an attorney. I found one through a customer from the bank. It was a difficult time for me as I had to meet with him and my husband and his attorney. And many times a judge was also present. They indicated that I had signed a document that stated that the home we bought together was governed under a family trust. I was not defined in the trust. I tried to prove that I never signed this document and that I had records to show the money I had put into the mortgage and furniture. I had a negotiator that tried to get some compensation for selling all my property in Wisconsin, leaving my family and trying to start over again, alone. He finally put his arm around me and said, "This man will only give you a small amount of money and the furniture." You must take this, as he will not give you any more. Then he said, "You're a pretty lady. You should have no trouble." On the drive home I couldn't believe what he said that to me. I finally settled, however, my ex-husband could not pay right away. So he lived with his girlfriend and I lived in the condo for about a year. Even though it was a difficult year; it gave me time to have my mind focused on Eric and his cancer treatments.

During that time I had another event about to happen that also tested my faith. The bank I worked at was sold to another bank and my co-workers and I knew some changes could happen. One day I was asked to come to the corporate office. I was to meet with a human resources woman from the bank that was taking our bank over. As I was seated in front of her desk, she said, "I have good news, and I have bad news. We have a position at our new bank for you. We will be closing the office you currently work out of." I thanked her and then she said, "All the other employees will be released." What we will have you do in a week is let each of them know and see if you can get them to stay and work during the next few months, before we close the office. If they all walk out when you tell them, we will close the office and bring you back to this office. Please don't let them know until we tell you when." It was late in the afternoon and my co-workers and I were going out after work. I called them, and they told me they would lock up and meet me at the restaurant. As I drove along, I was wondering how I would tell them. The only friends I had at this time, and in the next few months, we would be going in different directions. As I drove up to the restaurant, both Deanna and Iris were standing out in front waiting for me. They looked at my face and said, "We're losing our jobs and you're keeping yours!" I know they saw the shock on my face and I didn't have to say anything else. We put our arms around each other and went in to eat.

Once I explained to both of them about a bonus if they stayed until the office closed, they both stayed. We had several months to enjoy together before the office closed. At the same time, I was going through my divorce, Iris was going through one too. This helped me to heal from mine.

I found a cute little condo close to where Iris lived and it was time for me to move. Iris had a friend and another co-worker and her husband helped me. On a Saturday morning they brought trucks and cars and we filled them up and headed for my new home. By the end of the day, they all helped put all the furniture in place and all the pictures were hung on the walls. We laughed and had a good time. Then, they waved good-bye and I closed the door.

Suddenly, I was all alone! I had never experienced this feeling before. I didn't know anyone in the development. No children, no dog, no husband and no relatives in the area. I was scared. I asked God to watch over me and then I turned up the TV and looked out at the lake.

Iris and Deanna become family to me. Iris and I started looking for a church to go to and found the Spanish River Church. We became members and suddenly I had found new friends. Deanna's family began inviting me to their homes for the Holidays and also, their Jewish Holidays. They became my Florida family. My life started to become somewhat normal again. The stress of the divorce was gone. I could now spend my time praying for Eric.

At church each Sunday I filled a prayer card for Eric and put it in the offering plate. Many of the people who were praying for Eric would stop me and ask how he was doing. One Sunday I was seated next to a young woman. She saw me writing my prayer request and asked me if I had someone that had cancer. I told her about Eric and she asked me what kind of cancer. I told her small tissue sarcoma. She had a surprised look on her face and began to tell me that she also had sarcoma when she was 18 years old. She was given months to live. She underwent radiation and also was on experimental drugs. I met her when she was 23 years old and she had been in remission for 2 ½ years. Her name was Laura and she always asked about Eric when I saw her at church. One Sunday she asked for Eric's address. After Eric passed away, I found a letter she sent to him and she gave him encouragement and hope and told him to trust in the Lord, and lean upon him during these troubled times. She also told him she knew what he was going though.

These two years were full of events that I would have never believed would happen to me. I learned that when my life calmed down I could see that I had to take one day at a time and with God's help I would be able to get through this. I was no longer in control.

Friends that helped me in times of trouble, Iris, Deanna and I

CHAPTER 10 B

"Be devoted to one another in brotherly love. Honor one another above yourself."

Romans 12: 10

1992

My Elizabeth

As I walked to the mailbox, I heard the palms rustle overhead from the wind blowing through them. I opened the box with my key and saw two identical envelopes inside. They were from the church I attended, Spanish River Church. I saw my name on one of them and the other had the name Elizabeth Fischer. Who was Elizabeth Fischer? As I walked back, my neighbor was at her front door. I told her about the second envelope and asked if she knew an Elizabeth Fischer. She replied, 'You don't know Elizabeth? She lives in the end unit upstairs. Go meet her!' I rang the doorbell and a beautiful young woman answered the door. I told her I lived downstairs and when I got my mail, I also had received a piece of hers. I asked her if she went to Spanish River Church and she replied sweetly 'yes.' I told her I had been a member for several years. She invited me in and this was the beginning of a great friendship. She told me she was an art teacher at Boca Raton High School and I told her I was a banker. I could see her talent as I looked around her condo. Her artwork was everywhere. I told her we should go to church together. She smiled and agreed. When I turned to leave, I felt that I had met someone very special. I later learned my feelings were right.

The next few weeks and months we became friends. At the end of our work day we would meet and walk around our complex. We laughed and talked about our lives. She told me she was single and wanted to find a special man and get married. I told her I was divorced and I had a son that had cancer and I need to have her pray for him. We walked and talked and loved to sing:

> "Our God is an awesome God
> He reigns from heaven above
> With wisdom power and love
> Our God is an awesome God."

Our voices would break in joyous song and broke the late afternoon silence. We love to see the beauty around us and would stop and look at flowers and trees as the birds and butterflies flew around us. She came into

133

my life at a time when I was so upset and worried about my son. She was a gift! As we talked, I learned that she had a booth at the Spanish River Church Women's Christmas Luncheon each year where she sold her jewelry. I told her that I had made and sold jewelry in Wisconsin and had a lot of boxes full of my work. She told me that she would let me know when the church was taking registration for the booths. She let me know and together for several years we each had a booth and we enjoyed setting up and selling our jewelry. Hers was different than mine and we both enjoyed the successes we received.

One year Elizabeth told me she was going to start selling her artwork about the same time I was working at making Christmas ornaments and candles. We continued for several years and she always encouraged me. One day a customer came into the bank and told me they were moving and needed someone to adopt a white Persian cat. I asked Elizabeth if she knew anyone who would like a beautiful cat. She looked at me and said, "I would like him." I arranged the meeting and this beautiful cat became Claude Monet, a.k.a. Mr. C. This was the beginning of Elizabeth's new love. And I found that keeping my hands busy was helping me keep my mind from the constant worry of what might happen to Eric.

As I arrived home from my son's funeral, I opened my door and in the entryway I saw a beautiful arrangement of flowers. Then I saw the most beautiful sight – my son's artwork framed and beautifully displayed! It was from Elizabeth.

One day Elizabeth told me she was having an evening out with some friends. She was wearing a black leather skirt and looked exceptional. The next day she told me she had met a special man. His name was Alan. I could see in her eyes that she enjoyed being with him. With time it turned out to be her husband. I was proud to have been at their wedding. Elizabeth's wish had been granted.

As Elizabeth started her new journey, I was so fortunate to be included in her new life. She was always praying for me and helped my heart heal after Eric passed away.

Elizabeth and Alan had a son named Jonathan, aka John, and I was able to watch him grow up. One day Elizabeth called me and told me they were moving to Acworth, Georgia. My heart was sad, however, this did not take her out of my life. I love hearing her voice on the phone, and she and her family will always be part of my life journey.

Pictures of the booths we had at the Spanish
River Women Christmas Luncheon

Me and "my" Elizabeth at my daughter's wedding

CHAPTER 11 B

"But those who hope in the Lord will renew
their strength. They will soar on wings like
eagles, they will run and not grow weary,
they will walk and not be faint."

Isaiah 40: 31

Cancer Treatment
(September 1991)

A sarcoma is a cancer that arises from transformed cells of mesenchyme tissue origin. Malignant tumors made of bone, cartilage, fat, muscle, vascular, or hematopoietic tissues are considered sarcomas. High-grade sarcomas are mostly treated with surgery, chemotherapy and radiation therapy. Sarcomas affect people all ages. Approximately 50% of bone or cartilage sarcomas and 20 % of soft tissue sarcomas are diagnosed in people under the age of 35 years old.

This is what Eric was diagnosed with in September of 1991, a soft tissue sarcoma. This was discovered in a muscle in his lower left leg. He was hit by a hockey stick, which caused a hard growth to form. It was the size of a quarter. When his doctors examined it, they decided it had to be taken out. The growth was benign; however the tissues surrounding the growth were full of cancer. When the doctors did a body scan it was discovered that both lungs had over 52 spots of cancer. Both lungs had too much cancer to support a transplant. They expected his life to end around two years from the day we met with Doctor Batson.

Eric made the decision to join the Research Department at the University of Wisconsin. He signed the papers and his journey began. The first thing Eric had to have was a port inserted under his skin. They placed it under the left collarbone. A small pocket was created and then the catheter was inserted into a vein or artery. The port is a small disc about the size of a half dollar. The entry is raised and designed to receive a needle. This makes it quick and easy to give injections. The top of the port is the septum that is made out of self-sealing rubber. This means it can be punctured hundreds of time with a special needle. Each time after the injection it reveals itself instantly. A steel plate is under the septum so the needle cannot go all the way through the port. Attached to the base is a flexible tube called a catheter. The catheter is inserted into a vein or artery where the medicine is to go. The port can be used to draw blood for tests and to inject medications into the bloodstream. It may also be used for infusions, when large amounts of fluids are needed, such as a blood transfusion, intravenous antibiotics, intravenous chemotherapy, or intravenous nutrition. The port was inserted during a brief operation. The port had to be flushed about every two weeks and because the port was under Eric's skin; he could safely bathe, swim, and exercise. This made it easy for Eric to receive these chemotherapy treatments. It became a part of his body.

He would get many different types of research cancer treatments, and a few days later his white and red blood would be tested. Eric explained how this would work. He said the object of curing cancer was that the good cells had to eat up the bad cells, just like playing Pac-man. Each treatment was reviewed to see if that was happening. This went on for many weeks, and then they would scan his lungs to see if the many cancerous spots on his lungs would decrease or disappear. Several times he had somewhat of a slight change and it brought more assurance that the treatments were working.

Eric and I settled into a comfortable period as we called each other almost every day. He seemed to grow into this unexpected change in his life. Things around him seemed calmer and he always told me what he did each day. He loved fishing and went as much as he could. He would tell me about catching the same fish over and over and released it back into the lake. He called the fish "Charlie." He played hockey with his friends and started putting his talent of art into beautiful art pieces. He made artwork for his friends, his sister, his father, and for mother's day, he sent me a large picture of Rusty Wallace's race car. Many times on a Sunday afternoon when a Nascar race was happening, Eric and I would call each other and watch the ending. Always, we both cheered for Rusty Wallace. Eric loved watching the Packers and after the games, we would discuss the players and the game.

Eric would have a chemo treatment and then his body seemed to bounce back very quickly. After each treatment, he would have to go back and get his blood counts. Many times after his treatments he would spend a lot of time in the playroom with the younger children who had cancer too. He enjoyed playing with them. I have a "Thank you" card from the nurses on the children's floor signed by Audrey, Karen, Aggie, Sherry, Jan, and Andrea. He had given the playroom his Nintendo game and they were thanking him for that. He loved music and especially "The BoDeans" from Milwaukee, WI and Jimmy Buffet. "Good Things" by the BoDeans was one of his favorite songs. He sent me a tape of this song so I would always be able listen to it. Because I told him never to send me any gifts, he decided to start sending me things that he owned. One Christmas he sent me his tape deck along with all the taped music he liked. It was mostly the BoDeans and Jimmy Buffet. I still have the tape deck and the tapes. I still cry when I hear these songs.

One day Eric called and told me he wished he could go to the Milwaukee Summer Fest to hear Jimmy Buffet in concert. All of his friends were taking a bus to Milwaukee. He told me his chemotherapy was cancelled and he didn't get a ticket because of his treatment schedule. I hung up the phone and felt a hurt that only a mother can have and wished I could grant Eric his wish. The next day I went to work at the bank and I didn't realize that my face showed sadness. One of my customers asked me why I looked so sad. I couldn't hold back my answer. My son is terminally ill with cancer and he wants to go to the Jimmy Buffet concert in Milwaukee and I don't know what to do. I wish I could make this happen. His eyes had a look of sadness. I never told many people about my son, because of the difficulty in talking about it. He left and a few minutes later he came back. He told me that he called the Jimmy Buffet store in Key West and they will have a ticket for Eric at the front office at the Milwaukee Fest. He gave me a phone number and told me Eric should call and verify that they had it. I started to cry. I was so happy. I called Eric that night and told him. He was so happy and I was even happier than him. The next day this customer came back to the bank and gave me a box. It was from Margarita Ville. Inside was a white sweatshirt with "Air Margarita Ville", an airplane, and Key West, Havana, and Bimini on it. He told me he wanted Eric to wear it to the concert. It was a present from him. I sent it to Eric and he went on the bus with all of his friends on July 1,1992.

I sent a "thank you 'to Jimmy Buffet and a few weeks later I received a package at my front door. It was from Margarita Ville. Inside was a book titled "Where is Joe Merchant?" Inside the cover was this message, "To Eric. This should take you to paradise for a while. Keep fighting the good fight. Your pal, Jimmy Buffet." Also, he sent a letter to me telling me to send this book to Eric and hoped it would bring a smile to both of us during this difficult time. A letter to Eric was also enclosed. He told Eric he was sorry he didn't' get to meet him and thanked him for being a loyal fan. He hoped Eric would enjoy this book. He then ended by telling Eric his parrots are with him during his struggle. Fins up bud, your friend

Jimmy Buffet. Eric had framed a picture of Jimmy Buffet on his wall. Inside the glass was the ticket to the concert dated July 1, 1992. I still have that picture and Lisa and I have the books.

The BoDeans and Jimmy Buffet's music and books became the greatest therapy in Eric's life. Wherever I am, when I hear their music, I stop and think of Eric. Jimmy Buffet was a great part of Eric's therapy. Then, his artwork became a way for him to find a creativity that he had as a talent from the time he was very young. He always liked to draw and create. He continued this each day during his treatments from his bedroom. "Charlie" the fish he always caught now was an art piece. The terminator, Bart Simpson, Michael Jackson combined with Madonna, Michael Jordan, a side profile of Madonna, a picture of Lisa's car, two pictures of an Indian motif, for a friend of Lisa's. Then, a special group of art pieces for Lisa. These three pieces are about 3ft wide by 4ft tall and the three are of women in different poses. She has them on her walls and it shows the talent that he had. Many of his art pieces were given to his friends and they brought them back for his service.

For the next 2-½ years of Eric's life it was peacefully calm and he filled his days and kept his mind and fingers busy. I know that he must have also asked God, why me? However he never let us know that.

He couldn't go out in the sun for these two and half years because of his treatments. He was very pale however the rest of his body looked very healthy. No one could tell that he was fighting this battle. The one thing that he didn't want people to know is that he had terminal cancer, mostly because of how people treated him. They didn't know how to handle it and what to say, so he stayed mostly in his bedroom in the world that he made for himself. I was at a wedding that he was a groomsman, and a man came up to him and said you sure are pale. Did you drink too much last night? One of his friends spoke up and said he has cancer. The man was shocked. His friends watched over him. When he went out with them and especially when he didn't have his hair, they all wore caps and bandanas on their heads so no one could tell that Eric was suffering. It was the greatest help they could have given him. Eric lost his hair about four times and each time his hair got darker and a little curlier. He never complained about this.

The following year when I went back to Wisconsin to see him, he was looking and feeling very well. I had prayed every day and began to think Eric may be cured of cancer. Eric told me he was excited to learn that he qualified for a treatment that was called whole body hyperthermia. This is a cancer treatment in which the body temperature is raised from 98 degrees to 107.6 degrees. Eric had an information form he wanted me to read:

You have been diagnosed as having advanced cancer, which has spread and cannot be cured by surgery or irradiation. You may also have been treated with chemotherapy, but at this point in time, the cancer is not responding to this treatment. You are invited to participate in a research study combining two experimental therapies, a drug called Melphalan which is experimental when given by vein, and whole body hyperthermia (heat treatment). Laboratory tests and prior clinical experience with these two therapies suggest that the combination may prove to be an effective approach to treating cancer. You will receive a hyperthermia treatment to evaluate any side effects of hyperthermia alone and your response to sedation. About a week later you will receive Melphalan alone. It will be infused into a vein over 10 minutes. Three or four weeks later, the hyperthermia treatment will be repeated and Melphalan will be infused after the optimal heating has been achieved. Three of four weeks later, tests will be done to evaluate your response. If your disease has responded to treatment or is stable, you may be eligible to enter a maintenance phase during which hyperthermia and Melphalan would be given once every 4 weeks for a maximum of four additional treatments. If there is evidence that your disease has become worse, or if not in your best interest, the treatment would be stopped and other options would be discussed with you.

The radiant heat for the treatment is produced by a machine containing water (like a radiator). Prior to and during the hyperthermia treatment, you will be sedated with short-acting intravenous drugs to make you or comfortable and relaxed. Throughout the procedure, you will be awake or lightly sleeping. You will be placed in a box with your head remaining outside the chamber. When your body had been heated to the desired temperature (107.6 degrees) you will be removed from the box and covered with blankets to maintain a high body temperature. After 60 minutes, the blankets will be removed to allow you to cool down over about 45 minutes to normal body temperature (98.6 degrees).

Then a week later you will receive Melphalan alone. Although Melphalan is a commercially available for doctors to prescribe in tablet form, the intravenous form will be used in the study. Melphalan may interfere with normal production of blood cells making you susceptible to bleeding, infection, and anemia, allergic reactions with swelling, rash, and shortness of breath may occur and rarely be life threatening.

Your doctors and nurses will be checking you often to see if side effects are occurring. Medications can be given to keep many of these potential side effects under control. The side effects usually disappear after the treatments stop.

Eric told me he had already met with Dr. H. Ian Robbins who would be performing this treatment. He told me he had signed the consent forms and would be starting this treatment very soon. Eric also told me when he met Dr. Robbins as he waited in a room he heard nurses and other doctors greeting as he came down the hall. He said it was if someone like God was coming to see him. After Dr. Robbins left him he said all the doctors and nurses told him what a great doctor he was. Eric was very hopeful about this treatment and was very happy he was picked.

During the two and ½ years in the cancer research department he had many doctors and nurses taking care of him. Several of them he told me about. He had one nurse, Karen that he always spoke of and was special to him. Also, besides Dr. Robbins, he spoke many times about Dr. Spriggs. I wish I had all the names of the many doctors and nurses that helped Eric though his 2 ½ years from 1991 – 1994. You were all special to him!

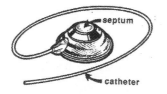

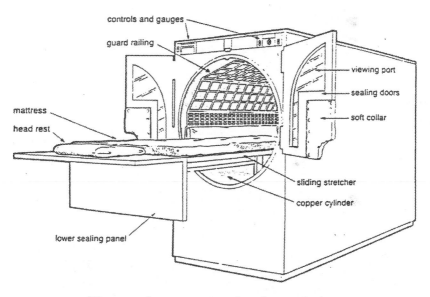

The port that was inserted under Eric's skin

The unit Eric was placed in for heating his body
as a part of the research treatments

CHAPTER 12 B

*"For this God is our God for ever and ever;
he will be our guide even to the end."*

Psalms 48: 14

Eric's Death
June, 1994

The phone rang and my daughter, Lisa answered it. I could see on her face something was wrong. She had come to Florida to visit me on her school break. I could see her eyes fill with tears. I whispered, "Who is calling" and she said, her dad. It was about Eric. I heard her say "I'll tell mom and will call you back." Once she hung up, she said "Mom, Eric's been put in the hospital." The doctors told her dad that it would be only a short time and we needed to come back to Madison. She told me that his breathing had worsened and he was getting weaker. Hospice had been contacted and his body was giving up. We should go to Madison as soon as possible. I told her I would change her flight schedule and I would also get my seat next to hers. We were scheduled to fly back on Saturday morning. The time had arrived that I was praying would never come.

As we journeyed to Madison, I was glad that Lisa was with me. She was able to keep me calm. When we arrived at the airport, her dad was there. He told us that we had to go right to the hospital. While we were driving, we were told that Eric had taken a sudden change in his breathing and the nurse told him that Eric was starting his transition to his end of life. The nurses and Hospice staff wanted to meet with us at the end of our visit. Eric smiled as we entered the room he was glad to see us. His body was very pale and oxygen was being given to him. I hugged him and could feel his bone structure. He seemed to have lost a lot of weight. We spent a few minutes with him and then a nurse asked to speak with us out in the hall. She indicated that Eric only had a few days to live. Since he was 24 years old, he had to make the decision on where he would like to be and he asked to go home to the apartment that Lisa and he shared. She told us that Hospice had been notified and a hospital bed had been ordered and oxygen tanks should be delivered on Monday. Also, they arranged to have a wheelchair for him to use. We could take him home on Monday. Hospice would be coming to the apartment later to talk with Lisa and myself, to give us information on the stages that he would be going through. We were all in a state of sadness, but we knew that this was what Eric wanted. We told Eric "Good Bye. I wanted to cry, however, I remembered what the woman at the airport had told me, "Don't you let him see you cry!"

We arranged the apartment so Eric would be as comfortable as possible. Soon, they came with the bed and we sat it up in the living room. On Monday we went to the hospital and brought him home. Then, a young man came to set up the oxygen tanks. I could see that he was about the same age as Eric and his eyes showed sadness as he put the tanks in place and set the oxygen level, and then left. We arranged the many bottles of pills that Eric had. Lisa numbered the caps and we went over his scheduled doses. I could see in his eyes he was glad to be in his everyday surroundings. Lisa and I sat up a schedule to make sure Eric had everything he needed. She had taken classes in the medical field and understood the medicine and when they need to be given. I sat with him and he looked up at me and said, "Mom, I wished you didn't have to see me this way." I held his hand and smiled back at him. Then he said, "Mom, don't ever stop smiling." I asked him if he was hungry and he said, yes. I went to the refrigerator and in the freezer I found several frozen dinners. I told him what I found and he said "Chicken Masala". He ate and then wanted to lie down on the bed. We helped him and again made him comfortable. The sound of the rhythm pumping of the oxygen became a part of the background that we heard each day. It became a part of the daily sounds.

Monday evening I slept on the sofa to be close to Eric. Lisa slept in her room. We were all tired from the moving and bringing Eric to the apartment. Tuesday morning Lisa made eggs and bacon and we all ate together. It was a calmer day, however, the seconds and minutes and hours seemed to be passing by very quickly. Hospice called us to see if we needed anything. They wanted to make sure we had read the information they had given us about the last stages of life. They questioned if they should come and be with us. Lisa and I decided we would be fine alone and we knew Eric didn't want other people to be around him. A couple of friends called to check on him and his step-brother, John, stopped by and I could see that Eric didn't want anyone to see him this way.

Around 4:00 the same young man came to check on the oxygen tanks and fill them. When he finished, I walked him to the door and he asked me to come outside. He told me that he had filled the tanks for the last time. Tears came to his eyes. He told me he would not be coming back. I hugged him and he walked away and I could see him wipe away his tears. I also wiped away my tears and went back through the door to attend to my son. I now knew that this would be the night that I would lose my son. My heart was breaking. I sat down on the bed next to Eric and I could tell he also knew what was going to happen. He said, "Mom, who will take care of Lisa?" I looked at him and said, "I will". Eric and Lisa had always had a close relationship and he always felt like her protector. I lay by him in bed and held his hand. He seemed to feel content and his breathing was more controlled. I heard my mind say, "Please Lord, watch over Eric and if you are taking him from us, make this easy for Lisa and me."

The evening was peaceful and suddenly Eric looked at me with a look of questioning. "Mom, they've come for me. Should I go with them?" I asked, "Who? Who has come?" "Three people in black robes are standing in the light. They want me to go with them. Should I go", he asked. I told him close your eyes and go with them. We love you and will miss you. Then he went into a peaceful sleep. Lisa got up and I followed her into the kitchen where we always would go if we needed to discuss something we didn't want Eric to hear. She asked me about who he was seeing. I told her I didn't know, but he was at peace. We went back and both of us sat by him as he slept. The evening seemed to go past so fast. We both knew from what Hospice told us and the book they gave us to read, that Eric was in the final stage of his life. As the oxygen level is decreasing, his lungs would shut down. We looked at each other knowing that this would happen soon. We could see on his feet and body that his skin color was turning blue from lack of oxygen. At about 9:30pm, Eric looked at both of us and said, "Thanks for all you've done for me. Then, he reached up to kiss each of us and said, "Good night, Mom", "Good night, Lisa", and he went back to a quiet sleep.

The evening seemed to go by very quickly and we could do nothing but wait. Lisa and I both sat on each side of him. We both were quiet as we were both in a state of shock. We could hear that his breathing was slowing down. It was about 4:00 a.m. on Tuesday morning that we heard a totally different breathing sound. At one point he opened his eyes and seemed to smile, then returned to his slow breathing. This continued until 5:28am when a last gasp took place and we could see that Eric had passed away. I asked Lisa to write down the time. We looked at each other and we were silent for a few minutes. I looked at Lisa and said, "Good-bye, Eric! We will always miss you."

Lisa and I got our thoughts together and knew that we needed to do something. I remembered that Hospice told us to call them, so I did. They told me to take a sheet and cover him. The lady talking with me told me she would call the coroner and she was concerned if we were okay. She told me that Hospice would be sending someone to come and talk with us. She told me to turn off the oxygen pump. Suddenly, the room was quiet. We both went into the dining area. I sat in the wheel chair and Lisa sat next to me. We couldn't talk, as we were both very sad. My heart was broken. We both felt a letdown. I felt every muscle in my body come back to life. We heard a knock on the door and it was the coroner. He went to the bed and checked Eric. Then, he brought in a stretcher and took Eric's body away.

Soon two Hospice women came and spent time with us. They wanted to make sure we were able to continue on with what we had to do to finalize the funeral arrangements that had to be made. They would help us with this. They asked to see Eric's pill bottles and took each bottle and counted the pills. I didn't understand and asked them why they had to do that. They said it was required, as they needed to make sure that nothing took place that would indicate he had been overdosed. I was in shock. What did they think? That we would take my son's life? They finished and told us everything was correctly given. What a relief, as Lisa and I were so worried that we might have made a mistake. They referred us to a funeral home and told us that they would make the arrangements for us. Lisa called her dad and told him when we were to meet. The three of us met at the funeral home and we decided to have Eric's body cremated. We wrote the article along with a picture and the funeral home was to put it in the newspaper the next day. My ex-husband, Bruce, reminded me about the site that we had purchased at a cemetery in West Madison several years before this. We had both forgotten the plots and agreed this would be where his body would be placed at rest. We decided to have a 'service of life' to honor Eric for what he had done in his twenty-four years of life.

Since Bruce, was a professional photographer and he had a large photo area that was immediately painted white where all of Eric's artwork was hung. After he passed away Lisa and I found stacks of artwork under his bed which we also displayed. All of his friends brought back the artwork that Eric had given them, so everyone could view them. We also placed his hockey stick, soccer ball, rollerblades, his fishing rods and one of his golf clubs in a corner. We hung his hockey shirt on his hockey stick.

During the time he was in treatment a trust fund was set up for Eric. He bought a computer with the money. We had it set up with a verse that let everyone know how we felt about Eric.

"God saw him getting tired and cure was not to be.
So he put his arms around him,
And whispered, come with me.
So he passed away
Although we loved him dearly,
We could not make him stay.
A golden heart stopped beating,
Hard working hands at rest,
God broke our hearts,
To prove to us,
He only takes the best."
      -Author unknown

The entryway had a picture of Eric and a cascade of Calla lilies, his favorite flower. A guestbook and several of his favorite things were on a table next to a photo book of pictures of his twenty-four years. The many flower arrangements started arriving and we placed them throughout the area where his artwork was displayed.

The service was Friday July 1, 1994 from 2-7pm. Both sets of grandparents drove together from Black River Falls to Madison to be at the service. It is about a 2-½ hour drive. They all had so much sadness on their faces. They all loved Eric so much. Lisa and Eric used to spend many summer with their grandparents.

The people started coming, friends, neighbors, relatives, Eric's high school and college classmates, nurses, doctors, and people who had heard of Eric and what he did in his short journey through life. At around 3PM the doors opened up and a group of Eric's special friends came through the door, all wearing white shirts and black slacks. Their eyes showed their sadness. Everyone viewed Eric's artwork and his accomplishments. So many people came.

After the service, Lisa and I went back to her apartment. Wednesday and Thursday we never left and during that time we felt Eric's spirit in the rooms. The first night a glowing light focused on his artwork. We looked outside and in the room, but we found no source of the ray of light. We still wonder about the light over the years that have passed. We were tired from the week and now this day ended without Eric.

Suddenly, we were awakened to Eric's alarm clock playing Jimmy Buffet's 'Brown-eyed girl.' We looked at each other in shock. His alarm clock had not gone off the whole week and now it was Saturday morning. Why did this happen? We stood looking at each other and we realized that Eric's spirit that we had felt had left us. His spirit that had comforted us in the last few days was now gone. It was as if the song was his good-bye to us. We will always remember this Farwell.

We spent Saturday going through his personal items. Inside his billfold I found a penny that had a heart pressed out of the center. I had sent Lisa and Eric each one in a Valentine card. He still had his. A tear came to my eye. We went through his clothes and I took his sweatshirt from Margarita Ville home with me. We both felt his absence in our life. His voice had stopped and his presence was gone.

The entrance to Eric's service
Jimmy Buffets picture
A grouping of Eric's favorite things

CHAPTER 13 B

"The moon and the stars to rule over the
night, for his steadfast love endures forever."
Psalms 136:9

My Final Years
Christmas Eve 2012

It was another Christmas Eve at Spanish River Church in Boca Raton, Florida. The years had passed very quickly. I looked over at my good friend Iris who also is a member of the church. We stayed friends for years and we always go to the Christmas Eve service together. Every year the service is full of Christmas beauty and the story of Christmas is always told in many different ways. Music and colored light, Christmas songs and candle lights always take place. Christmas was suddenly different for me starting in December 1994. The year Eric passed away, joy seemed wrong, especially at this time of the year. As the service ends, we always sing Silent Night and they dim the lights as we all hold lit candles. And when the line 'sleep in heavenly peace', I raise my candle higher and said, "Merry Christmas, Eric". Tears filled my eyes, but I felt a comfort that he was still with me. I have continued this for all the years that followed. Then in July 2, 2002 my father passed away and I wished Eric and dad Merry Christmas. This followed for many years and tonight it is a year that has taken more of my family. My brother Dallan passed away in January. On June 28, 2012 my mother passed away. Tonight as I raise my candle and the words 'sleep in heavenly peace', I wish Eric, Dad & Mom and Dallan a Merry Christmas.

As the song ended, I looked over at Iris, tears were again in my eyes. Iris had just lost her mom and I could see that she was missing her mom too. The years had gone so fast. Eighteen years had passed, during all these years Iris and I have spent much of our spare time going to movies and we liked traveling around Florida. On Christmas Eve we always meet before the service for dinner and always find a restaurant that is decorated in a festive way and we always sit outside and enjoyed the warm evening breezes. We always looked forward to this evening and we both felt that this night was what Christmas should be all about – Mary, Joseph, and baby Jesus. Over the years we both attended many women's groups and attend church on Sunday mornings. I will always remember all the prayer requests I made every Sunday during the 2-½ years of Eric's treatments. It was always the same, "Please pray for my son Eric during his battle with cancer."

The star was always an important part of Christmas. After Eric passed away I name a star in the sky in honor of him. The location of the star is:

Constellation – Hydra
RA 0847m 44.50SD-05 59' 57.192
Magnitude MV 10.9
Star #-12 4876 519

The name of this special star is 'Forever Eric', because this star will forever shine in the sky. This star is registered and the name is permanently filed in the Registry's Vault in Switzerland.

I know that Mary also followed the path of the nighttime sky and would remember how the special star directed the wise men to her special son Jesus.

Christmas is also a time for gifts, and the most special gift I received was at Christmas several years after Eric had passed away. One day after church, I came home and lay on my bed. I was still struggling with why Eric was taken from me. Did I do something wrong? Why couldn't I keep him from getting cancer? As I lay there, I turned over and my arm knocked my Bible on the floor. I usually kept my Bible in the top drawer of the desk next to my bed. I looked down at the Bible and as I picked it up, the book was opened to 1 Corinthians 15:35-58. I read it over and over and then realized what God wanted me to know. This was the beginning of my complete healing along with learning about Mary's journey and my journey. I knew that I now understood what spiritual life was about. (This scripture is in the preface of this book)

"We bring nothing at birth; we take nothing with us at death. The Lord alone gives and takes. Praise the name of the Lord." Job 1:21

Spanish River Church in Boca Raton, Fl

CHAPTER 14 B

*"Honor your father and your mother
so you may live long in the land the Lord,
your God, is giving you."*

Exodus 20: 12

January 28, 2008
(Honoring My Mother and father)

As I drove home from work, I was thinking about another birthday was over. Time seems to go faster as you get older. I stop to get my mail and I had several birthday cards from my friends and family along with a large envelope from my mother. My mother never forgot my birthday. I opened the envelope and inside was a diary with a picture of a little girl and boy. A key hung down and inside was what I always wished for. The best gift of all. I had told her about the book I was writing and wanted to have her tell me her story. My mom and dad didn't talk much about their lives. As I got older, I realized what a great life they had given me. I never heard my parents swear or have anger in their voices. They always provided for my brothers and me. We never felt poor. They made sure that we were raised with Christian values. We went to Sunday school and to weekly church youth organizations (MYF). My mom was about 89 years old when she wrote this. I took the key and unlocked the diary and this is part of what followed in her handwriting:

YOU ASKED…WITH LOVE, MOTHER.

I, Laverne Tilda Lubow, was born November 30th at home in Kenyon Valley, 1918.

It was hard times and we were raised on a farm. My parents were Henry and Bertha Lubow. I had three brothers: Ernest, Arnold, (myself) and Virgil the youngest.

People in these days were poor. Jobs and money were short. People on the farm raised cows, chickens and your had your own meat and milk.

You needed good horses. They pulled all the machinery. Our family had a good apple orchard and a good garden. Everyone in the family worked together and canned food to last through the winter. Grown up children lived with the family. In the summer they would work for a neighbor, with his crops. They would get food and a bed and a small amount of money. (Fifty cents a day pitching hay) There weren't many jobs to be had.

A lot of children never finished 8th grade. The family made all their clothes.

People cut firewood and sold it to make a living or traded it for winter clothes for the family. Wool underwear was always needed. The winters were so cold. You couldn't buy things you have today.

We went to a one-room school in Kenyon Valley. We all went through 8ᵗʰ grade and Virgil and I went to High School. We walked 8 miles a day to go to school. I stayed a week or two in town and my mother paid with milk and eggs. The lady kept asking for more because she had more kids. All year around she used the eggs and milk to feed her family. She always made a pudding that saved her some money.

After High School, I worked as a maid, helped take care of 4 kids and did housework. Most of the girls had to take those jobs. There was nothing else to do we worked for our board and 3 or 4 dollars a week. Families worked hard, and had to work together to live.

We canned, or stored, our vegetables in the cellar. We canned our meat, made dried fruit, and made jelly. 'Made our bread and baked everything we had to eat. We had a big apple orchard so we always had apples that we wrapped in paper and stored all winter.

We had an old cheese factory in the valley and the people cleaned it up and had dances and parties. All the kids learned how to dance and the whole neighborhood would turn out for picnics. Then the young people started growing up and leaving the Valley. There started to be more jobs and better pay.

When the cheese factory stopped, my brother and his friend John played music for the Lodge Hall of Komensky. Ernest took his girlfriend and 2 or 3 of us girls. We'd dance all night. There was a dance every Saturday night in the old ZCBJ in Komensky. Now, the Hall is near Black River Falls. There was always a crowd. There was a young man that always brought a neighbor girl down to dance with.

One night he came alone. He asked me to dance a couple of times. The next Saturday he came alone and asked me to dance. After a few Saturday nights he asked me to dance and during that dance he asked if I would go on a date with him. He took me to the movies. He took me home and asked if I would go again. So I went again. When we got home, he asked if we could talk. He would like to know more about me. He asked if I was one of those girls who went out and had sex before going home. I said I didn't want that. He said good because I don't want that either because I don't want to get in trouble and have to marry and live with a woman all my life that I didn't want to live *with. So we started going together knowing what we both wanted out of life, picking the person we want for life. We kept going out together that summer and one night when he took me home, he asked me if I would marry him, but don't answer now, he said, think it over. If all I can make is $45.00 a month, you will be poor all your life. That was what most men made a month at the time. He was the nicest man I had gone with. He had respect for women and old people and would talk things over, so I answered yes the next time we went out. We started planning for a wedding. I sent to a mail-order house for my dress and veil. We got everything taken care of and we set the date for July 16th, 1938 in Humbird, WI at 10 o'clock. My brother, Arnold, and Bob's Niece Elaine Sharp, from Antigo stood up for us.*

Bob and his brother built a little one-room house. Then Bob's folks passed away and we moved in to the house. Bob's brother Louis was building a new house in the city, BR Falls, and when the war was on and Louis was called to duty. He asked Bob if he would trade for the small farm and he would sell the farm before going into the service. So we moved to town. A couple years later, my mother passed away and my dad came to live with us. But, he didn't like town and talked Bob into buying a farm. So that's what he did. We still have the house in Kenyon Valley.

You, Dallan and Dennis went to the Kenyon school until they moved you kids to town school and you rode the bus.

We farmed for years and your dad got sick. The doctor told him to stop farming and work 5 days and rest up over the weekend.

Dallan and Dennis were out of school and you were finishing up. Dallan went to school in Minn. One year and later left for California and Dennis had your dad sign so he could go into the Navy. He was only 17 years old.

I was still working at Anthony's store and then I went to work at Norplex. I worked that job until they closed the plant. By that time you had married Bruce and had a family.

When we started out, we had our paychecks but no back up money. Your dad had his dad's tobacco jar, glass with a gold metal top and fancy bottom, so we started putting our small change into it. When it was full, your dad took it to the bank. There wasn't enough for a CD so he put the money into Savings so we started saving again. Then we got our first CD so we kept on saving small change and got a few more CDs, so we had a little backup. We both worked until we retired. After that we got to spend all our time together

There was a time when all the people in the Valley would go from house to house. They would bring something to eat every Saturday night we would go from one house to the other. The children would play and the parents played cards. The people who owned the house would make coffee and they had good desserts. Years later, now the people who were young tell about the good time they had at these parties.

When we retired, your dad liked to play horseshoes. He and his friends played at night after supper. Sometimes the ladies went along and visited and talked while the men played. We both went once a week for groceries and your dad took care of the household supplies.

Bob had mouth troubles and he went to the doctor and the doctor sent him to Marshfield. They operated and it was cancer. So I drove him every day to Marshfield for a treatment, every day for 30 days. We never missed a day.

We stopped at Borufka's garage to get an oil change and your dad went out to look at the new cars, came back and said, "I found a car I want". It was the car I still have, a 1985 Buick. Your dad said, he'd have it made if he could buy a new car, pay and take it home. He did. He wrote 2 checks and took the car home. I still have it. The best used car in the country.

Your dad was good for years and when he had his yearly checkup they found a white spot on his liver and said they must watch. He had to go back every once in a while so they could keep a close watch on it. The last time they said they couldn't do anything more for him. Your dad left us July 2, 2002. The funeral was July7 and a few days later on the 16 was our 64th wedding anniversary. I can't remember what else happened in July but it was a bad month for me. Now I must make all decisions and wonder if I I'm doing them right. You never know what life brings you. But you must make your own heaven on earth.

Your dad and I always talked things over and worked things out. You have to buy things you need and save your money, not everything at first and then you can't pay. Couples don't work together nowadays. They each work, and they each spend the money. Their kids raise themselves. They don't know how to cook, wash the clothes; they have to eat out at all times. They do as they please.

Now that I'm alone, I buy only what I need. We have so much in the house I guess I don't need anymore.

Now I'm going to do the things I didn't have time to do, and I mow the lawn, and have my garden, and I water and trim the flowers at the cemetery a few hours a week. This winter has been the worst in the last seven years. It's cold - 40 degrees below in Jackson County with a cold wind.

I was lucky to get a husband like your dad. Many people today are greedy and want everything for themselves. Now I'm almost 90 years old and you kids took me out for supper and brought me a birthday cake.

Now is the time for me to try new things, and I'll try to make things better. You have to be thankful for what you have. Things could be worse!

With Love,
Your Mother

My mom and dad retired and they never stopped working. Dad set up a workshop in the basement and became a carpenter. He made about 7 grandfather clocks. He gave one to each of us in the family, and we think he made several more for friends. He also built cabinets and other wooden items that they used in their household. He worked in the garden and kept the yard mowed. He still loved to watch the Green bay Packers on television and enjoyed the easier life that he was given. The last time I saw my father was the summer before he passed away. He was having some health issues and he was 86 years old. My mom and daughter and my two granddaughters were in the garden. I was sitting next to my father. He looked at me and said "You're not going to see me again as I'm sick, however, I want you to know that I know how difficult your life has been. The one thing I want you to do is never stop smiling". He said that life is not always fair. When you're young and you never have money that you wish you did, and then when you're older you have money when you don't really need as much. I always wished we would have had more money when you and your brothers were younger. I looked at my father with tears in my eyes and gave him a kiss. That summer was the last time I saw my father. .

My mother also kept busy during her retirement. She loved to crochet table cloths and she made quilts for each of us. She also loved to paint artwork, which she taught herself. She entered the county fair each year and won many ribbons and awards over many years. In the last few years they were together they gave some of the items from their household to the museum in Black River Falls, Wi. Mom's wedding dress and shoes and dad's suit are on forms for generations to see. They also gave many of their pictures of events that happened during their lives.

Mom would meet many of her church friends every Friday morning at the cemetery. The cemetery during the summer had many live flowers. Most parts of the cemetery had no water available. They all carried pails of water to the sites and made sure the flowers were watered. It was especially important for her to continue doing this to the area that dad and her brothers were all laid to rest. Dad and mom had purchased their sites many years before their passing and hers was beside his. Her name and date of birth were there for her to see. The date of death was blank.

Mom stayed on the farm for about six years after dad passed away. She always was at the front door when we all met at the farm, always over the 4th of July. My brother Dennis and his family and I and my family would make the trip to the farm. She always had the table full of food and greeted us with her famous cinnamon rolls and apple pie.

She was always happy and she loved to work hard on her pride and joy, her giant flower garden. She kept the lawn mower with a push lawn mower and she tended the vegetable garden and still used the produce to eat. She also planted pumpkins for the grandchildren at Halloween. She had many friends that called her and made sure she was okay.

We soon got word through a young farmer, Dale, and his wife, Vonnie, that mom seemed to be having a change in her memory. They were farming the land around mom and dad's house and always stopped to make sure she was able to take care of herself. My brother Dennis found a retirement home near Blaine, MN where he lived and we moved her there. It was difficult for her to leave the farm but soon found an easier life where she was now taken care of.

Mom passed away June 28, 2012 at 93 years old exactly 10 years after dad's death. She is now at rest next to dad. Once again, I was flying home over the fourth of July for her service. It still is a mystery to me that Eric passed away June 29th, Dad July 2, and Mom June 28 and I found in mom's bible that my grandfather passed away July 5th. For years we all met at the farm over the 4th of July and it was if we were all to be together for each of their farewell services.

Mom's service was filled with many of her friends and family. We all knew that this was now going to be the end of the days at the farm. My brother's and I grew up there. My children Lisa and Eric spent summers and Holidays there. My grandchildren Christina and Caitlin loved going to the farm also. It was a part of all of our family's lives. Mom and dad had everything written in their will as to what they wanted. The farmhouse and land around it they wanted the young farmer Dale and his wife Vonnie to have the first chance to buy, if none of us wanted it. They had sold some of the land to them a few years before dad's death. My mom and dad had worked all of their lives and left us many blessings.

At my mom's service, Pastor Kathleen from the Methodist church read the following verses. Mom and dad had attended this church and were some of the first members of the church.

She picked these verses and this was my mother and a wonderful tribute to her. Proverbs 31:10-28

A wife of the noble character,
Who can find?
She is worth far more than rubies,
Her husband has full confidence in her,
And lacks nothing of value.
She brings him good, not harm,
All the days of her life.
She selects wool and flax
And works with eager hands.
She is like the merchant ships,
Bringing the food from afar.
She gets up while it is still dark,
She provides food for her family,
And portions for her servant girls.
She considers a field and buys it.
Out of her earnings she plants
A vineyard.
She sets about her work vigorously
Her arms are strong for her tasks
She sees that her trading is
Profitable, and her lamp does not go out at night.
In her hands she holds the distaff.

And grasps the spindle with her fingers. She opens her arms to the poor and extends her hand to the needy. When it snows, she has no fear; her households for all of them are clothed in scarlet. She makes coverings for her bed; she is clothed in fine linen and purple. Her husband is respected at the city gate, where he takes his seat amount the elders of the land. She makes linen garments and sells them, and supplies the merchants with sashes. She is clothed with strength and dignity. She can laugh at the day to come. She speaks with wisdom and faithful instructions are on her tongue. She watched over the affairs of her household and does not eat the bread of idleness. Her children arise and call her blessed, her husband also, and he praises her. Many women do noble things, but you surpass them all. Charm is deceptive and beauty is fleeting but a woman who fears the Lord is to be praised. Give her the reward she has earned and let her works bring her praise at the city gate.

After my mom died, the house was cleaned up and all of my parent's items were divided between us children and family. We each took things we wanted as keepsakes. I wasn't able to be there, but Lisa found things that she knew I would want to have. I have my mom's Bible, and when I first picked it up it broke in half. She had it filled with information about our family and items saved from memories she had. As I opened a box of pictures, I found an envelope dated May 8, 1968. I opened it and in my own handwriting I found…

Dear Mom and Dad,

Sunday night after you left, Bruce and I went back in the house and just sat for an awful long time. We decided we wanted to somehow tell you both thank you for everything you've done for us. 'Thank you' doesn't really seem like enough.

As we sat there we thought about all the things that our folks had given us since we were old enough to understand. I can remember mom when you sat up all night sewing a dress for me and somehow it seemed like I just didn't appreciate all the work you put into it. I always seemed to find something wrong.

Also, the times when I was told 'no', I couldn't go to something just because everybody else was going. But, I can look back now and realize all these things were helping me become the person you wanted me to be. I feel fortunate that you both gave me the chance to know how to work for things I wanted by picking strawberries and beans and doing jobs around the farm. I learned that you don't get things like cars and houses by just wanting them.

I remember the day dad bought me that used peach-colored bicycle with my strawberry money. I hopped on, and with guiding hands, he gave me a push and I went wobbling down the road. Soon I got my feet going and I got everything under control.

Sunday, when we were planting the flowers and the shrubs you brought, we realized all the guidance and love and patience plus all the material things… I know as those shrubs and flowers grow, we'll always remember Sunday. We both hope someday we'll be able to help our son or daughter in the same way you've helped us reach such a dream. I know this will be the biggest year of our lives and one we won't forget. Being able to live in such a beautiful house and have our first child all at once seems like a wonderful dream, but we both know it is only coming true due to the wonderful parents that we both have.

Love as ever,
Bruce and Sandy

Pictures of my parents wedding day, clocks my father made,
an art piece my Mother Painted, along with the telephone
we had and the tobacco jar they used for saving money.

CHAPTER 15 B

"Blessed are the peacemakers,
for they will be called children of God."

Matthew 5:9

Final Chapter
Counting My Blessings

God who watched over me and guided me and Mother Mary for her story which helped me heal. Now and through this journey the spiritual growth given me at Spanish River Church (Boca Raton, FL)

My mother and father who raised me in a Christian way

My daughter, Lisa, who traveled part of this journey with me

My grandchildren Christina and Caitlin that are such a joy to me

Elizabeth, who came into my life and helped me become closer to God. She will always be a special blessing to me.

Iris and Deanna who helped me through each day during some of the hardest, forging life-long bonds

Deanna's Jewish family and her son, Max, who brought a family setting into my life, and who shared with me their faith

Jimmy Buffet for giving Eric inspiration to create artwork, through his songs and books

To all the good Samaritans that came into my life and into Eric's life, along with all the doctors and nurses. Also to all my friends in Madison Wi and in Boca Raton, FL

The 24 great years with Eric

As I finish this book, I realize that if mother Mary wrote down her blessings, they would be almost the same as mine. She was such a blessing to me as I journeyed along with her and the many experiences she had in her life journey.

In the years that followed, life was somewhat calm for me. Then the news came to me that Lisa after having two children, Christina and

Caitlin was diagnosed with thyroid cancer. After surgery and radioactive treatments along with being quarantined from her family during these treatments, she is ten years cancer free. Once again I went through the questioning, why both of my children had cancer. However, I thank God for helping us through these challenges.

One day when I was in my early sixty's I looked out the door of my office and I saw a strange man pacing up and down in front of the door. At 4 o'clock he walked into my office and told me my job was eliminated. I looked at him and said "who is going to run the bank." He told me not to worry about that. He walked me to my car and as I left the bank, I felt like a criminal and didn't know what I had done. I cried as I drove home and thought about all the work I had put into opening this branch bank. I not only helped set up the teller line but also helped staff the office and I brought in customers, some I knew from previous years in banking. As I arrived home, my phone was ringing and one of the mangers from another office told me she too lost her job. Her name was Lorraine and she had just lost her husband. We both were shocked and scared and felt unsure about what was happening. We both were about the same age and could only believe it was about our age. They didn't need us anymore. We both had to file for unemployment which made us feel terrible, as we both always worked hard and never needed to ask for help. As the days passed, it only got worse as many of my friends and customers from the bank called me and kept asking me what I did wrong. This was a hard time for me, as I felt after 25 years in banking my career was taken away from me and I didn't know why. Also, for the first time I felt old and I was no longer needed. It was weeks later that we found out that the bank out of Jacksonville Fl was closing all of the offices in the south Florida area. We both could not believe why they treated us this way. This was a difficult time for me; however, I found another job and worked on. Once again I prayed to God for help.

One of the greatest lessons I learned as I wrote this book was that both Mary and I enjoy the same every day sights. The rising and setting sun that I view each morning and evening was the same sun she saw. The beautiful evening sky and stars that I still delight in were the same stars and night sky she viewed and used for guidance along her travels. The clouds that I enjoy and spend so much time watching were also in her daily life. The birds singing and breezes blowing that I enjoy so much, were a part of her life too. I also thought of Mother Mary's life two thousand years ago as very cruel and difficult in the way people treated one another. I see around me in my lifetime people are still having the same difficulties, children shooting innocent children, husbands and wives not finding happiness in their marriages, people cheating one another for money, countries still battling over territories and vying for power and wars that kill innocent victims.

I learned that God wants us to have peace and happiness even though we suffer with a loss of our loved ones and difficulties we encounter in our lives. I still think about the words both my son and father told me before they passed away, "never stop smiling." The smile that I thought would never come back, I now have. I feel that God, Jesus, and the Mother Mary brought peace and happiness back to me, my family, and my friends.

"The Lord gives strength to his people; the Lord blesses his people with peace." Psalms 29:1

My wish to each of you that read this book is that you will be given much peace and happiness and many blessings from God. Amen.

Last picture taken of Eric and me, a few months before he passed away

Whenever I feel sad and troubled and wonder why Eric had
to die, these words come to me and I find my answer.

<u>Let It Be</u> – The Beatles

When I find myself in times of trouble
Mother Mary comes to me
Speaking words of wisdom
let it be

YOU ARE NOW ENTERING
THE ART GALLERY OF;

Three artworks of women that are 4 feet by
5 feet, Eric especially made for Lisa

From women series, Michael Jordan
Michael Jackson and Marilyn Monroe faces combined,
Madonna and From his Women series

These were all gifted to his friends

Nascar driver Rusty Wallace's car, 3 feet by 4 feet, this was
gifted to me on Mother's day the year before he passed away.

An art piece that he created of Lisa's red Mustang

Charlie the fish and the
bait he caught him with

Looking out the window
from my rocking chair

Two Indian art pieces
that his father has

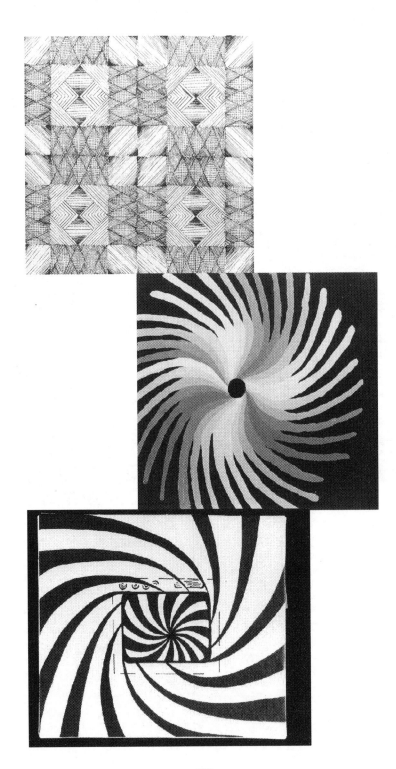

179

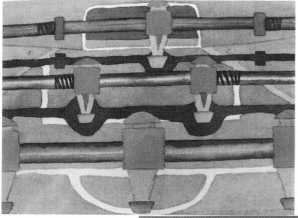

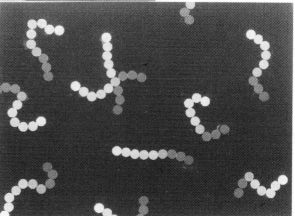

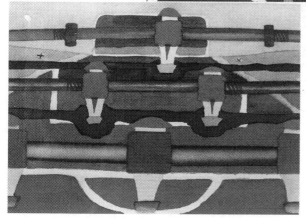

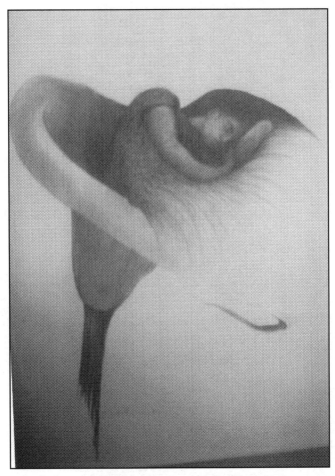

"Sleep in heavenly peace"
This art piece of Eric sleeping in his favorite flower a calla lily, was created by "my" Elizabeth Fischer, and gifted to me after his death.

Printed in the United States
By Bookmasters